OUR DAILY BREAD FOR KIDS

KIDS®

90
Jesus & Me Devotions

written by
Crystal Bowman & Teri McKinley

illustrated by
Anita Schmidt

Our Daily Bread
Publishing®

To my children, grandchildren, and those still to come—may
you follow Jesus all the days of your life.
—C. B.

To the Belsky family—may you grow in the grace and
knowledge of our Lord Jesus Christ.
—T. M.

To my grandma. Without your faith I would never have
found mine.
—A. S.

Our Daily Bread for Kids: 90 Jesus & Me Devotions
© 2025 by Crystal Bowman and Teri McKinley
Illustrations by Anita Schmidt. © 2023 by Our Daily Bread Publishing

Excerpted from *Our Daily Bread for Kids: 365 Devotions from Genesis to Revelation,* Volume 2 © 2023.

Requests for permission to quote from this book should be directed to: Permissions Department, Our Daily Bread Publishing, PO Box 3566, Grand Rapids, MI 49501, or contact us by email at permissionsdept@odb.org.

ISBN: 978-1-64070-417-6

Design by Jody Langley

Printed in the United States of America
25 26 27 28 29 30 / 6 5 4 3 2 1

Introduction

Did you know that the Bible is the bestselling book of all time? More than six billion copies have been sold since the printing press was invented by Johannes Gutenberg in 1440. But the Bible is really a collection of sixty-six smaller books that have been divided into two groups called the Old Testament and the New Testament. It's more than just a collection of exciting stories though. Together, those sixty-six books tell *one* big true story.

This collection of ninety devotions from *Our Daily Bread for Kids* volume 2 will help you learn more about the Bible and how much God loves you. But what makes these devotions extra special is that whether the Bible passages we look at are from the Old Testament or the New Testament, they all point to Jesus. You'll have a special moment with God each day and grow closer to Him as you learn more about who Jesus is and all He did.

The words *Our Daily Bread* come from the prayer Jesus said when He was teaching His disciples how to pray. In Matthew 6:11, Jesus prayed, "Give us today our daily bread" (NIV). Just as we need to eat food every day for our bodies to be strong, we need "spiritual food" to have strong belief and trust in God. As you read the devotions and open your Bible, ask God to help you understand what He wants you to know so you can be spiritually strong.

You can read the devotions on the following pages by yourself or have a grown-up read them with you. You might want to read this book with your family at mealtime or bedtime. However you use it, our prayer is that you will learn how much God loves you and how Jesus makes a way for you to be a part of God's family.

Are you ready to go on an unforgettable journey through the Bible? Let's get started!

Crystal and Teri

If you come across words you don't understand, look them up in the glossary at the back of the book.

Jesus Was There

Then God said, "Let us make human beings in our image and likeness. And let them rule over the fish in the sea and the birds in the sky. Let them rule over the tame animals, over all the earth and over all the small crawling animals on the earth." —Genesis 1:26 ICB

The story of creation tells us how our world began. On the sixth day God said, "Let us make human beings in our image and in our likeness." Did you notice the word *us*? Who was God talking to since there were no people?

There is only one God, but He exists in three persons—Father, Son, and Holy Spirit. Genesis 1:2 says that God's Spirit was hovering over the waters. A verse from the New Testament says that Jesus is exactly like God. Jesus is higher than all things. God created everything through His Son (see Colossians 1:15–16).

TALK TO GOD
Thank God for making you in His image.

The Son is Jesus, who is also God. He made the sun, moon, and stars appear in the sky. He made the plants and trees on the land. He created whales to splash their tails and eagles to soar through the sky. He watched tigers race across the land and koala bears climb gum trees. So when God said, "Let us make human beings in our image," the word *us* refers to the Father, Son, and Holy Spirit. This is called the *Trinity*, which means "three in one."

Because God made people in His "image," we can know God in a way that's different from the rest of creation. He created us with a spirit so we can talk to Him and learn about Him from the Bible and from His creation. God created the world by speaking words, but He created a human being by breathing life into him. The first person was made in God's image, and so are you.

EXPLORE MORE: Read Genesis 2:7 to find out how God created the first person.

Jesus is my creator.

DID YOU KNOW?
The cheetah is the fastest animal on land and can run up to 70 miles (113 kilometers) per hour.

Adam and Eve in the Garden

The Lord God gave the man a command. He said, "You may eat fruit from any tree in the garden. But you must not eat the fruit from the tree of the knowledge of good and evil. If you do, you will certainly die." —Genesis 2:16–17 NIrV

God named the first man Adam, and he was different from the rest of God's creation. Unlike the animals, Adam could talk to God, and God talked to Adam. God made Adam perfect in every way. But it wasn't good for him to be alone, so God created the first woman, Eve. God placed them in a beautiful garden called Eden. The garden had rivers, trees, and animals. God wanted Adam and Eve to take care of the garden and enjoy it. He told them to eat the delicious fruit from all the trees—except for one. But one day, Adam and Eve ate fruit from that tree. For the first time, they disobeyed God— the Bible calls that sin—and that changed everything. Now they had to work hard for their food, and they would experience sickness, pain, and death.

Adam and Eve were sorry they didn't listen to God. But God still loved them even though He had to discipline them. God knew that all people would sin, so He made a way for their sins to be forgiven. As time went on, God asked people to bring their best lamb or goat as an offering, or sacrifice, to Him. This would make things right between them and God for a while. But it was something they needed to do over and over again, because they kept on sinning. They would need a lot of lambs or goats!

TALK TO GOD
Ask God to help you do what is right, and thank Him for making things right through Jesus.

Today we still disobey God, but we don't have to bring God sacrifices anymore. God loves us so much that He gave His son for our sin instead of lambs and goats. When Jesus died on the cross, He gave His life for us and paid for all our sins. His sacrifice was enough to last forever! Jesus's sacrifice is all we need to be right with God, and believing in Him as our Savior gives us eternal life.

EXPLORE MORE: Read Genesis 3:21 to find out what God made for Adam and Eve after they sinned.

DID YOU KNOW?
In the English language, the name Adam means "man." It comes from the Hebrew name Adamah which means "land" or "red earth."

Jesus makes things right.

Noah Builds an Ark

Noah had faith. So he built an ark to save his family. He built it because of his great respect for God. God had warned him about things that could not yet be seen. . . . Because of his faith he was considered right with God. —Hebrews 11:7 NIrV

The story of Noah's ark is a well-known story from the book of Genesis. You may have heard it at church or read it in one of your Bible storybooks. Perhaps you drew a picture of the ark with giraffe heads peeking out of the windows. God told a man named Noah to build a huge ark for him and his family. God also told Noah to take two of every animal and bring them into the ark. That's why the ark had to be big!

This story takes place many years after God created the world. The people had turned away from God and didn't listen to Him anymore. Genesis 6:6 says that God was sorry He put people on the earth. He decided to wash everything away in a flood except for Noah and his family, because Noah loved and obeyed God.

Noah believed what God said even though he didn't understand everything. Noah built the ark just like God told him to. When Noah finished the ark, he and his family went inside. The pairs of animals went into the ark too. Then God closed the door. The rain poured down and flooded the earth. The ark kept Noah and his family and the animals safe because Noah had faith in God.

TALK TO GOD
Ask God to give you faith to believe in Him.

Do you know how Jesus is like the ark? Jesus can keep us safe too. When bad things happen in the world, we can trust in Jesus to help us. Jesus protects us from danger just like God protected Noah from the flood. It takes faith to believe because, like Noah, we don't always understand everything in our world. The next time you hear the story of Noah and the ark, remember that God keeps us safe. We can be like Noah and trust and obey God.

EXPLORE MORE: Can you guess how old Noah was when the flood was over? Read Genesis 8:13 for the answer.

God keeps me safe.

DID YOU KNOW?
Some people think there were as many as 30,000 animals on the ark.

A Big Surprise

"Is anything too hard for the Lord? I will return to you at the appointed time next year, and Sarah will have a son." —Genesis 18:14 NIV

Abraham was one of Noah's distant relatives who loved God very much. One day he was sitting under a tree when he saw three visitors walking toward him. He bowed to greet them and offered to get water to wash their feet. In those days people wore sandals and walked along dusty roads so their feet were often dirty. Abraham told his wife, Sarah, to bake some bread, and he told his servant to prepare some meat for the visitors to eat.

As Abraham talked with the men, they had some surprising news! They told Abraham that Sarah was going to have a baby the following year. Sarah was listening, and when she heard the news, she laughed because she was way too old to have a baby.

TALK TO GOD
Thank God that He can do impossible things.

Many years before, God had promised Abraham that his family would become a great nation. Abraham didn't see how that could happen since he and Sarah didn't have any children and he and Sarah were old. But God kept His promise, and Sarah had a baby boy one year later. Abraham named him Isaac, which means laughter. The huge family God promised to give Abraham would come through Isaac.

When things seem impossible to us, we need to remember that God can do anything. He is not limited like we are. When He says something is going to happen, it will. The Bible is filled with God's words and promises, and we can believe they are true.

Almost two thousand years after Isaac was born, another baby boy was born who was also promised by God. He is one of Abraham's distant relatives, a descendant, and His name is Jesus.

DID YOU KNOW?

In Abraham's day, sandals were made from leather or wood. People used leather straps to tie them to their feet.

EXPLORE MORE: What does Psalm 127:3–4 say about children?

God can do things that are impossible for us.

A Long Hike

Abraham answered, "God himself will provide the lamb for the burnt offering, my son." And the two of them went on together.
—Genesis 22:8 NIV

Abraham was filled with joy when his son, Isaac, was born. Years later, God told Abraham to go to the region of Moriah and take Isaac with him. Abraham must have been sad and confused when God said the purpose of the trip was to offer Isaac as a sacrifice, just as people offered animals to God. How could God ask Abraham to give up the son He had promised?

Abraham trusted God and did what God asked even though he didn't understand. After walking for three long days, Abraham saw the place where God wanted him to build an altar. When Abraham placed the wood on the altar, Isaac asked, "Where is the lamb for the offering?" Abraham told Isaac, "God will provide the offering."

Abraham tied Isaac to the altar. But as he raised his knife, an angel of the Lord called out, "Abraham! Do not harm your son! Now I know you love God more than anything else."

Abraham looked up and saw a ram caught in the bushes. Instead of his son, Abraham sacrificed the ram. Abraham named that place The Lord Will Provide. The angel told Abraham that because he obeyed God, he would have many descendants. And people throughout the world would be "blessed," or cared for and happy, because Abraham obeyed God.

TALK TO GOD
Tell God how much you love Him.

This story of Abraham and Isaac is a symbol, like a picture that shows us what our salvation is like. The Lamb that God provides for our sacrifice is Jesus, His one and only Son. In the New Testament, John the Baptist said that Jesus is "the Lamb of God, who takes away the sin of the world" (John 1:29). Through Jesus, every person can have salvation.

EXPLORE MORE: Read Genesis 22:16–18. How did God describe the number of Abraham's descendants?

God will provide.

DID YOU KNOW?
In the days of Abraham, altars were made of dirt or stones found in a field, and no tool could be used to make them.

What's Your Name?

God said to him, "Your name is Jacob. But you will not be called Jacob any longer. Your new name will be Israel." So he called him Israel. —Genesis 35:10 ICB

When we meet someone new, the first thing we ask is their name. Names are important because they tell others who we are. Some people are named after relatives or famous people. Some parents give their kids a name just because they like it. Names have meanings, too, and many people like to find out what their name means.

In the Bible most people only had first names. A person would be called, "Isaac, son of Abraham," or "Jacob, son of Isaac." We also read in the Bible that God sometimes changed a person's name. God changed Abram's name to Abraham, and Sarai's name to Sarah. In the New Testament, Jesus changed Simon's name to Peter. In the story of Jacob, we learn that God changed his name to Israel.

God promised Jacob that his descendants would become a great nation. Since his name was changed to Israel, his sons were known as the sons of Israel. His descendants were known as Israelites.

Today people have a first and last name, and most people have a middle name. Our last name tells what family we are from. Different cultures have different ways of naming their children, but every culture believes names are important.

TALK TO GOD
Thank God for being your Father.

Another name we can have is the name Christian. People who are Christians are followers of Christ. Any person can be called a Christian if they believe that Jesus is the Son of God who died to forgive our sins. If you are a Christian, it means that God is your Father, and you are part of His family. It's the most important name of all!

EXPLORE MORE: Read Genesis 17:3–6 to find out why God changed Abram's name to Abraham.

DID YOU KNOW?
The name Jesus means "God saves us."

My name is important.

Waiting for God's Promises

Wait for the Lord. Be strong and don't lose hope. Wait for the Lord.
—Psalm 27:14 NIrV

When God promised Abraham his descendants would be as many as the stars in the sky and the grains of sand on the shore, Abraham didn't even have a child. But the promise God made to Abraham continued through his son Isaac, his grandson Jacob, and the Israelites. Hundreds of years later, God's promise came true. Jacob's family arrived in Egypt with around 70 people. By the time the Israelites left, there were more than 3 million people, and the numbers kept growing.

TALK TO GOD
Thank God for keeping His promises.

When Jacob and his family moved from Canaan to Egypt during the famine, God told Jacob that he would die there, but God would bring his descendants back to Canaan. Four hundred years later, God chose Moses to lead the children of Israel out of Egypt. That was the beginning of their return to Canaan and the fulfilling of God's promise.

In the Old Testament, God also made many promises of a Messiah, and those promises came true when Jesus was born two thousand years later. It's exciting to read the Bible and see how many of God's promises came true, even if it took hundreds or thousands of years.

The Bible is more than stories about people who lived a long time ago. The Bible is God's Word to us, and many of His promises are for us today. God promises to listen when we talk to Him, and He promises to answer our prayers. But sometimes we need to wait for His answers. As we read the stories in the Bible, and see how God's promises always come true, we can trust God to keep His promises.

EXPLORE MORE: What did Moses bring with him out of Egypt? Read Exodus 13:19 to find out.

God keeps His promises.

DID YOU KNOW?
Joseph was seventeen when he went to Egypt.

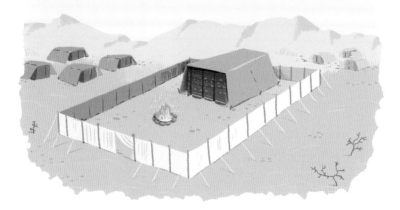

The Israelites Build a Tent

"The people must build a holy place for me. Then I can live among them. Build this Holy Tent and everything in it by the plan I will show you." —Exodus 25:8–9 ICB

In the book of Genesis, we learn how God gave Noah special instructions for building an ark. God told Moses to build something, too, but it wasn't a giant boat. God told Moses He wanted the Israelites to build a tent where they could meet with Him. This tent was not the kind people use when they go camping. It was known as the Holy Tent or tabernacle, and it would be God's dwelling place.

God gave instructions on how to build the tent and what needed to go inside. He asked people to bring offerings of gold, silver, bronze, fine linen, and purple and red thread. They also needed to bring cloth made from goat's hair, olive oil for lamps, sheepskins, and acacia wood. The people could give as much or as little as they wanted. They were so excited to give that they brought more than enough.

TALK TO GOD
Thank God that you can meet with Him anywhere.

The yard around the tent was where the people offered sacrifices to God. The tent had two rooms: the Holy Place and the Most Holy Place. A thick curtain separated the two rooms. Only the priests were allowed in the Holy Place. Only the leader of the priests, called the *high priest*, was allowed to enter the Most Holy Place.

Did you know that the tabernacle was a symbol for Jesus? When Jesus was born, God came to earth in human form. Jesus's body was like a tabernacle where God lived. When people met with Jesus, they were also meeting with God. If you believe in Jesus as your Savior, then God also lives in you.

DID YOU KNOW?
The people were able to move the tabernacle because it was "portable." Whenever the people moved to another place, they would take the tabernacle down and set it up again.

EXPLORE MORE: What colors of yarn were used to make the curtain for the entrance to the courtyard? Read Exodus 27:16 to find out.

God lives in His people.

The Priestly Blessing

The Lord said to Moses, "Tell Aaron and his sons, 'This is how you are to bless the Israelites.'" —Numbers 6:22–23 NIV

Moses's brother, Aaron, was a high priest. As the high priest, he was the head of the other priests. The priests would offer special sacrifices in the outer courts of the tabernacle and ask God to forgive their sins and the sins of the people. Then they would enter the Holy Place to meet with God.

The priests wore special clothes. The priests would speak to God for the people. Then the priest would give God's words to the people.

TALK TO GOD
Thank God that because of Jesus you can talk to Him and enter His Holy Place.

One day God spoke to Moses and gave him words for the priests to say to the people. These words are called "the priestly blessing," and many church leaders still say these words today. The blessing is found in Numbers 6:24–27:

> The Lord bless you
> and keep you;
> the Lord make his face shine on you
> and be gracious to you;
> the Lord turn his face toward you
> and give you peace.

God told the priests to say these words to the people so His name would be on them. This meant that God would bless them because they had His name with them.

Did you know that Jesus is our High Priest? Jesus made an offering to God for the sins of all people by sacrificing His body on the cross. Because of Jesus, we don't have to make a sacrifice before speaking to God, and we don't need a priest to speak to God for us. Because of Jesus, we can talk to our holy God ourselves. His name is with us, and He blesses us.

EXPLORE MORE: What does Hebrews 4:16 tell us about approaching God?

Jesus is my High Priest.

DID YOU KNOW?
The priestly blessing is also known as the "raising of the hands." When a priest or pastor gives the blessing, they usually raise their hands.

All Those Names!

"Your name will be Abraham, because I have made you a father of many nations. I will greatly increase the number of your children after you. Nations and kings will come from you." —Genesis 17:5–6 NIrV

It's exciting to read Bible stories about God's amazing miracles—like when He parted the Red Sea or broke down the walls of Jericho with the shouts of His people. It's also fun to read stories of how God provides for His people in unusual ways—like sending manna from heaven or having birds bring food to Elijah. But when we get to chapters 1–9 of 1 Chronicles, many readers could be tempted to skip those chapters. Who wants to read pages and pages of names that are hard to pronounce?

You might wonder why all these names are in the Bible, but there is a reason they are included. Way back in the book of Genesis, God promised Abraham that he would be the father of many nations, and kings would be among his descendants. This long list of names shows that God kept His promise to Abraham. It also shows that Abraham's descendants came from other nations, and not just the nation of Israel. This list of names ties the Old and New Testaments together, and when we read other lists of names in the Bible, they show us how Jesus came through Abraham's family line.

TALK TO GOD
Pray that people all over the world will come to know Jesus as their Savior.

The lists of names that lead to Jesus include people from different countries and nations. God's plan of salvation is for everyone who believes in Jesus as their Savior. It doesn't matter what country your great-great-great grandparents came from. What matters is that you love God with all your heart and believe that Jesus came to forgive your sins.

It's hard to count how many kings descended from Abraham, but the greatest King is Jesus!

EXPLORE MORE: According to Psalm 67:1–3, who should praise God for His power to save us?

DID YOU KNOW?
The list of names found in 1 Chronicles 1–9 includes 130 names that begin with the letter *A*, 110 names that begin with the letter *J*, and 105 names that begin with the letter *S*.

There are many nations in God's family.

Nobody's Perfect

Surely there is not a good man on earth who always does good and never sins. —Ecclesiastes 7:20 ICB

Ever since sin entered the world through Adam and Eve, no one can live a perfect life. Even a great leader like Moses did what he wanted to do instead of what God told him to do. We often hear the phrase "nobody's perfect," and it's true.

God gave the Israelites the Ten Commandments to protect them and keep them safe. He wanted them to know how to love God and other people. If they followed God's commandments, things would go well with them. If they didn't, they had to face consequences for their actions.

TALK TO GOD
Ask God to help you do the right things.

It's impossible for us to live a perfect life. That's why God sent Jesus. Jesus was human, but He is also God's Son, so He never sinned. When He died on the cross, He took the punishment for all the sins of the world. When we believe in Him, the wrong things we do are forgiven. We will never be perfect on earth, but that's how God sees us when we become part of His family.

Even though God forgives our sins, we need to ask Him to help us live in a way that shows our love for Him. When we choose to do what we know is wrong, we may face consequences. Cheating on a test will get you in trouble at school. Being mean to other kids will keep you from having friends, and lying to your parents will make it hard for them to trust you.

The Bible teaches us how to love God and love others. We may not be able to do it perfectly, but God will help us when we depend on Him.

EXPLORE MORE: What does 1 John 1:8–9 tell us about sin?

God loves me even though I am not perfect.

DID YOU KNOW?
The Bible and scientists agree that telling the truth is good for your health.

Where Is Your Home?

But our homeland is in heaven, and we are waiting for our Savior, the Lord Jesus Christ, to come from heaven. —Philippians 3:20 ICB

The world is a very big place where billions of people live. With seven continents and 195 different countries, there are many places people call home. Some families spend most of their lives living in one area of the world. They may grow up with sisters and brothers, grandpas and grandmas, and dozens of cousins who live close by. Other families move around because of jobs or because they want to live in warmer or cooler areas.

Families who serve in the military move to different places where their service is needed. Missionaries move to other countries to tell people about Jesus. Some families like to live in the mountains, and others want to live near an ocean. But no matter where families live, they all want to have a place they call home.

TALK TO GOD
Thank God that someday we can live in heaven with Him.

The Bible tells us that our homes on earth will not last forever. If we believe in Jesus, then we have a forever home in heaven where we'll live someday. We don't know everything there is to know about heaven, but we do know it's more wonderful and beautiful than we can imagine. Not only that, it's always light in heaven because God is there. In heaven, no one gets sick or hurt. No one is sad or afraid. Heaven is only filled with good things.

The Bible tells us about some amazing people like Abraham, Moses, and King David who lived long ago. Someday, when we get to heaven, we will meet them and many other great people! We will dance on streets of gold and sing songs of praise with the angels. Heaven is the best home in the universe!

EXPLORE MORE: What did Jesus say about heaven in John 14:2–4?

DID YOU KNOW?
Antarctica is the coldest continent in the world. Scientists work at research stations in Antarctica for short periods of time, but no one else lives there because it's covered with ice.

Heaven is my forever home.

David Becomes King

"Please, bless my family. Let it continue before you forever. Lord God, you have said these wonderful things. With your blessing let my family be blessed forever." —2 Samuel 7:29 ICB

The Israelites were at a place called Hebron when the time came for David to become their king. The people told David, "We are your family. Even when Saul was the king, you were the one who led us." Then they made David king of Israel.

David was thirty years old when he became king. In 2 Samuel 7 we read how God spoke to David through the prophet Nathan. He said, "I have taken you from tending sheep in the pasture to being the leader of my people. I am with you everywhere you go, and I have helped you win your battles. Now I will make your name famous and will provide a homeland for my people. Your son will build a temple for me, and his kingdom will be strong. Your family and kingdom will continue forever."

TALK TO GOD
Ask God to bless your family.

King David responded by praying to the Lord, "God, you are great! There is no one like you! You have made Israel your very own people, and you are our God. I am your servant. Bless my family with your promise, so it will continue forever."

More than a thousand years later, Jesus was born into the family line of David. When God made this promise to David, He was talking about the kingdom of God that would last forever through Jesus. When we believe that Jesus is the Son of God who died on the cross for our sins, we become part of God's forever kingdom. Jesus is the King who rules over the entire world. No king will ever be greater than He is!

EXPLORE MORE: Who else said, "I am the Lord's servant"? Read Luke 1:38 to find out.

Jesus's kingdom lasts forever.

DID YOU KNOW?
About six hundred years before David was in Hebron, Abraham bought land in Hebron for four hundred pieces of silver.

True Words

All your words are true. All your laws are right. They last forever.
—Psalm 119:160 NIrV

Many people believe in God, but not everything they say about God is true. Job's friends said that God was punishing him for doing something wrong, but that was not why Job was having problems. We need to be sure the things people say about God are true.

If someone tells you that God doesn't love you, that is not true! When people say that the Bible is full of stories that people made up, that's not true either. We know everything written in the Bible is true, so we can believe what we read. The prophets, kings, and disciples of Jesus who wrote the Bible were guided by the Holy Spirit. They wrote down the words that God told them to write.

When Jesus came into the world, many Old Testament prophesies were fulfilled by Him. Details of His birth, His teaching, and His death were predicted in the Old Testament. When they came true, it showed we can trust what the Bible says. We can also believe every word that Jesus said because He is God. Jesus not only spoke what is true, He is the truth. In John 14:6 Jesus says, "I am the way and the truth and the life. No one comes to the Father except through me."

TALK TO GOD
Ask God to help you learn what is true.

The way to know if something is true or false is to study the Bible and search for the answers to your questions. If you don't understand something, ask God to show you. You can also talk to a parent, pastor, or teacher who understands the Bible. It's impossible for God to lie, so we know every word He says is true!

EXPLORE MORE: What did Jesus tell His followers in John 8:31–32?

DID YOU KNOW?
In some courts of law, witnesses place their hands on the Bible and promise to tell the truth.

God's Word is true.

The Good Shepherd

The Lord is my shepherd. He gives me everything I need.
—Psalm 23:1 NIrV

A shepherd's job is to take care of sheep. Shepherds make sure their sheep have everything they need. They give the sheep food and water. They watch over the sheep while they sleep to make sure nothing happens to them. They show the sheep the right way to go and bring them back if they go the wrong way. When sheep travel through dangerous areas where they might get hurt or another animal might attack them, the shepherd keeps them safe.

King David knew all about a shepherd's job because he was a shepherd when he was young. Before he became king, David watched over his father's sheep in Bethlehem. Later on, he wrote Psalm 23, which is one of the most famous passages in the Bible. It is also called "The Shepherd's Psalm." In Psalm 23 David writes about a good shepherd who takes care of his sheep. He says, "The Lord is my shepherd. He gives me everything I need." In his poem, the Good Shepherd is Jesus.

TALK TO GOD
Thank Jesus for taking care of you like a good shepherd.

As David thought about taking care of sheep, he realized that God takes care of His people the same way. Like a shepherd, Jesus provides for us. He gives our souls peace, like a lamb lying down in the grass. He shows us the right things to do, like a herd of sheep walking on the safe path away from danger. Even when we go through hard times, we don't have to be afraid because Jesus is with us. He is like a shepherd with a staff that will keep us safe. Jesus is the kindest shepherd, and He loves us like shepherds love their sheep.

EXPLORE MORE: What does Jesus say about himself in John 10:11?

Jesus is the Good Shepherd.

DID YOU KNOW?
The first shepherd in the Bible was Abel, Adam and Eve's son.

A Different Kind of Priest

The Lord has made a promise. He will not change his mind. He has said, "You are a priest forever, just like Melchizedek." —Psalm 110:4 NIrV

Have you ever heard of a man named Melchizedek in the Bible? You might be thinking, *Melchiz-a-who?* His name is first mentioned in the book of Genesis when Abraham rescued Lot after being captured during a war. When Abraham returned home, he was blessed by Melchizedek who was called "priest of God Most High."

Melchizedek was a priest, and he was also a king. In the Old Testament, someone was either a priest or a king but not both. Melchizedek doesn't stand out as an important character in the Bible until we start reading about Jesus. In Psalm 110, David remembered God's promise to always let his family rule. Jesus came to earth through David's line and is a King and Priest, similar to Melchizedek. Let's find out what that means for us today!

TALK TO GOD
Praise Jesus for being the greatest High Priest and for being alive in heaven to talk to God for you.

In the Old Testament, we read about the high priests who came from the family of Aaron and the tribe of Levi. Their job was to talk to God for the people and to offer sacrifices so God would forgive their sins. But Melchizedek was born hundreds of years before Aaron, which means he was another kind of priest. He was a king and priest of a higher order than other priests. Jesus is not like the other priests either. Jesus was made Priest by God's power, and He will be a Priest and King forever.

God sent Jesus to sacrifice himself for our sins. That's why we don't need to make sacrifices anymore to be forgiven. Being a high priest like Melchizedek means Jesus is our King and High Priest forever, and He never changes. What a great High Priest!

EXPLORE MORE: Read Hebrews 7:1–3 to find out more about Melchizedek. How is he like Jesus?

DID YOU KNOW?
Some of the hardest names to pronounce in the Bible are Maher-Shalal-Hash-Baz (found in Isaiah 8), Zaphenath-Paneah (found in Genesis 41), and Cushan-Rishathaim (found in Judges 3).

Jesus is the greatest High Priest.

As White as Snow

"Even though your sins are bright red, they will be as white as snow.
Even though they are deep red, they will be white like wool."
—Isaiah 1:18 NIrV

Isaiah was a prophet to the people of Judah for more than fifty years. We can read his writings in the book of Isaiah, which is one of the longest books in the Bible. The name Isaiah means "the Lord saves." Isaiah brought messages from God to the people of Judah so they would be sorry for their sins and follow God.

TALK TO GOD
Ask God to help you follow Him, and thank Him for forgiving your sins.

God told Isaiah He was angry that the people of Judah no longer obeyed Him. They pretended to serve Him by celebrating festivals and making sacrifices, but God could see that their hearts were far from Him. Isaiah gave the people strong warnings about what would happen if they continued to sin against God.

Even though God was angry with their sinful ways, He was always willing to forgive them. Their sins were like a deep red stain, but God said He would remove their sins if they agreed to follow and obey Him. God promised to make their hearts pure and clean. He would wash the stains of their sin and make them as white as freshly fallen snow or like white wool.

God wants us to follow and obey Him, just like He wanted the people of Judah to follow Him. Turning away from God leads us away from Him and the good plans He has for us. But when we follow God, He will shower His love on us and give us the blessings that come with being close to Him. If you love and follow God, He will forgive your sins. And no matter how big the stain is, He can make it as white as snow.

EXPLORE MORE: What did God tell the people to do in Isaiah 1:16–17?

God will wash away my sins and make me clean.

DID YOU KNOW?
Isaiah's words are quoted in the New Testament more than any other prophet. Many of his messages are about Jesus, the Messiah.

Many Names for Jesus

His name will be "Wonderful Counselor, Powerful God, Father Who Lives Forever, Prince of Peace." —Isaiah 9:6 ERV

Isaiah lived about seven hundred years before Jesus was born, but God gave him messages that came true when He sent Jesus to earth. Isaiah shared this message: "The Lord will still show you this sign: The young woman is pregnant and will give birth to a son. She will name him Immanuel" (Isaiah 7:14).

Do you know who God was talking about in this message? The young woman was Mary, and the Son was Jesus. The name Immanuel means, "God with us." It was an important name given to Jesus because when Jesus lived on earth, He was God in a human body.

TALK TO GOD
Thank God that the Bible tells us what Jesus was going to be like before He was even born.

Isaiah wrote about other names Jesus would have too. His name would be Wonderful Counselor because He would be kind and loving and teach people about God. He would be called Powerful God because He would heal people who were sick, cast out evil spirits, and raise people from the dead. He would be called Father Who Lives Forever, because He would be a Father to all who believe in Him. And His name would be Prince of Peace because He would bring peace to the world (Isaiah 9:6).

Isaiah said God's Son would rule with love and fairness forever. When Jesus was on earth, He loved everyone and taught them how to love others. Now He rules from heaven, and someday He will come back to rule on earth—forever. God gave these messages to Isaiah, who gave them to the people. They were written down so that hundreds of years later, when Jesus was born, people would know He was the Messiah. Today we can read these messages in the Bible and believe that Jesus is the Son God promised to send.

EXPLORE MORE: Read Luke 1:30–33 to learn of another name Jesus would be called.

DID YOU KNOW?
There are more than fifty different names for Jesus in the Bible.

Jesus's names tell us who He is.

God's Spirit Is in Jesus

A branch will grow from a stump of a tree that was cut down. So a new king will come from the family of Jesse. —Isaiah 11:1 ICB

Many verses in the book of Isaiah talk about Jesus. We know from other Bible passages that Jesus would be born into the family of David, and today's verse from Isaiah 11 says it again. The "branch" from the family of Jesse, David's father, is Jesus, and He would bring new life to a dying kingdom.

In this chapter, the verses tell us how Jesus would have God's Spirit in Him and be filled with wisdom. When Jesus was on earth, He spoke with wisdom and had the right answer for everything. We can learn from His wise words in the Bible and ask Him to give us wisdom as we live and learn.

TALK TO GOD
Ask God to give you wisdom as you read the Bible to learn more about Jesus.

Jesus was also filled with understanding. He understood the needs of people who followed Him, and He understands our needs too. Jesus wants us to come to Him with our problems because He understands how we feel and has the power to help us.

Verse 3 says that Jesus would not judge people by the way they look. He would find joy in obeying God and always do what was right and fair. When Jesus was on earth, He was kind to the poor and loved everyone. He healed people who couldn't walk. He placed His hands on people with skin diseases to make them better. He helped a blind beggar to see, and let little children come to Him. Jesus still loves people today and wants us to follow Him just as we are.

God gave Isaiah these words to write so people would know that Jesus is the Son of God, filled with the Holy Spirit, who came to save us from sin and teach us how to live.

EXPLORE MORE: What does Luke 2:39–40 tell us about Jesus when He was a young boy?

Jesus is filled with God's Spirit.

DID YOU KNOW?
A tree stump can grow back to a full-size tree if the roots are still alive. If there are enough nutrients left in the roots, a sprout will grow from the stump.

A Light for the Nations

And now he says, "You are a very important servant to me. You must bring back to me the tribes of Jacob. You must bring back the people of Israel who are still alive. But I have something else for you to do that is even more important: I will make you a light for the other nations. You will show people all over the world the way to be saved." —Isaiah 49:6 ERV

One of the most amazing things about the Bible is that it is one big story. It's not a bunch of separate stories bound together in the same book. The things that happen in the Old Testament are part of the story of the New Testament, and the other way around. Isaiah 49 is one of the places where we see a connection between the Old and New Testaments in the big story of God's Word.

In this part of Isaiah, God is talking about the Messiah who would come to save Israel. And God tells us that He had an even bigger plan than that. The Savior of the Israelites would be the Savior of the entire world! God said, "You will show people all over the world the way to be saved."

TALK TO GOD
Thank God for sending Jesus to save you and people from all over the world.

By reading stories in the New Testament, we learn the Messiah is Jesus. And we know that Jesus didn't just come to save the descendants of Israel—He came to save all of us. As we go through more of the Bible, we will see the ways Jesus reached out to people who weren't Israelites and how He helped His disciples get ready to tell people all over the world about Him.

From the beginning, God's plan was for Jesus to save people from every part of the world. God said Jesus is a light to all the nations. Aren't you glad that Jesus is shining His light in your life? We all get to be a part of God's big plan by believing in Jesus as the Savior of the world.

EXPLORE MORE: What did Jesus tell His disciples in John 14:6?

DID YOU KNOW?
The Bible is the most widely read book all around the world. It has been translated into more than seven hundred languages.

Jesus came to save people all over the world.

The Suffering Servant

After his suffering he will see the light, and he will be satisfied with what he experienced. The Lord says, "My servant, who always does what is right, will make his people right with me; he will take away their sins." —Isaiah 53:11 ERV

A prophecy is when God tells someone about something that will happen in the future. God told Isaiah many prophecies to write down. Some of the prophecies in the book of Isaiah are about what would happen to the Israelites for disobeying God. And some prophecies describe what Jesus would be like and what He would do when He came to earth.

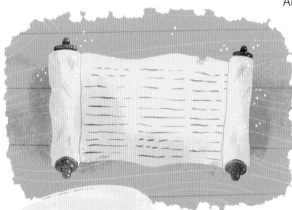

Isaiah 53 is one of the chapters that is all about Jesus. All twelve verses tell us about Jesus hundreds of years before He was born. God told Isaiah that there would be nothing special about the way Jesus looked to make us notice Him. He said that people would make fun of Him, and they wouldn't accept Him. He would also know what it was like to go through pain and sadness.

TALK TO GOD
Thank God for His plan to send Jesus to save you. And thank Jesus for loving you so much that He died for you.

And then God told Isaiah exactly why Jesus was coming and what would happen to Him. Isaiah said, "But he was being punished for what we did. He was crushed because of our guilt. He took the punishment we deserved, and this brought us peace. We were healed because of his pain."

God said His Servant, Jesus, would take away our sins by giving His life for us.

Jesus was willing to go through all that pain and suffering because He loves you. It was worth it to Him to be mistreated and hurt because it would give all of us the chance to be made right with God. It's amazing that God told us about that before it even happened. And it's beautiful that Jesus loves us so much!

EXPLORE MORE: What did Jesus say about giving His life for us in John 10:17–18?

Jesus makes me right with God.

DID YOU KNOW?
Some people who study the Bible believe there are more than three hundred prophecies about Jesus in the Old Testament.

The Good Branch

"In those days and at that time, I will make a righteous branch sprout from David's family. He will do what is fair and right in the land. At this time Judah will be saved. The people of Jerusalem will live in safety. The branch will be named: The Lord Does What Is Right." —Jeremiah 33:15–16 ICB

As you've seen in other books of the Bible, Jesus shows up everywhere! The book of Jeremiah is no different. In Jeremiah 33, God tells us a little more about the promised Messiah, Jesus. God told Jeremiah, "The time is coming when I will do the things I promised. I made a special promise to the people of Israel and Judah." And then God starts talking about a righteous branch that would grow from David's family. God told Isaiah about this branch too. God said this "branch" would do what is fair and right. The people of Judah would be saved by this branch, and the people of Jerusalem would live in safety. The branch would be named The Lord Does What Is Right.

TALK TO GOD
Thank God that He always keeps His promises and that you can trust Him to do what He says.

God was not talking about an actual branch from a real tree. But have you ever heard of a family tree? It's a graph that shows how people are related to each other. God was saying that Jesus would be a part of King David's family tree. That's important because it shows He is part of a royal family, which means He is a King. And it shows that He was born into a human family, which means He was a real person in addition to being God.

God promised that all this would happen. He said it was as sure as how day and night always come at the right time. Then the Lord told Jeremiah, "Someone from David's family will always sit on the throne and rule the family of Israel." That person is Jesus, the King who will rule forever!

EXPLORE MORE: What did Jesus call himself in John 15:5?

DID YOU KNOW?
The longest family tree recorded belongs to the Chinese philosopher, Confucius. His family tree has more than eighty generations and goes back over 2,500 years.

Jesus is the righteous branch.

Three Days inside a Fish

When Jonah fell into the sea, the Lord chose a very big fish to swallow Jonah. He was in the stomach of the fish for three days and three nights. —Jonah 1:17 ERV

When the sailors threw Jonah into the sea, he sank to the bottom. Seaweed wrapped around his head, and he was sure that he would die. But God was not finished with Jonah and wanted to give him a second chance. God sent a big fish to swallow Jonah, and Jonah quickly learned that he could not run away from God.

When Jonah found himself inside the belly of a giant fish, he cried out to God. He finally made a promise to God and said, "I will give sacrifices to you, and I will praise and thank you. I will make special promises to you, and I will do what I promise. Salvation only comes from the Lord!"

TALK TO GOD
Thank God for second chances, and ask God to help you listen to Him.

Jonah was inside the fish for three days and three nights. Then God told the fish to spit out Jonah onto the shore, and it did. The Lord spoke to Jonah again and said, "Go to that big city Nineveh and say what I tell you." This time Jonah obeyed and went to Nineveh.

Many of the stories in the Old Testament point to Jesus, and this is one of them. Matthew 12:40 says, "Jonah was in the stomach of the big fish for three days and three nights. In the same way, the Son of Man will be in the grave three days and three nights." When Jesus died on the cross, His body was placed in a tomb. But three days later He came back to life to show that He has power over sin and death. And like Jonah said, "Salvation only comes from the Lord!"

EXPLORE MORE: Read part of Jonah's prayer in Jonah 2:5–7.

God gives us many chances to obey Him.

DID YOU KNOW?
Great white sharks, groupers, and sperm whales are large enough to swallow a human. The largest fish known is the whale shark, which could swallow a human too.

A Message for the Future

"But you, Bethlehem Ephrathah, are one of the smallest towns in Judah. But from you will come one who will rule Israel for me. He comes from very old times, from days long ago." —Micah 5:2 ICB

Micah was a prophet who received messages from God in the form of visions. He lived around the same time as Isaiah and Hosea, and his messages were for both Israel and Judah. Jerusalem was the capital city of Judah, and Samaria was the capital city of Israel. Micah's messages were the same as the messages from other prophets, "Turn back to God or be captured by your enemies."

The people didn't listen to Micah. Israel was captured by the Assyrians, and Judah was captured by the Babylonians. But like the other prophets, Micah also gave a message that someday God would make everything right.

As you know from other passages, many stories and verses in the Old Testament point to Jesus. In the book of Micah, about seven hundred years before the birth of Jesus, we learn that Jesus would be born in Bethlehem.

Bethlehem was a small, unimportant town in Judah. It was also known as the City of David because that's where King David was from. Many verses in the Old Testament tell us the Messiah would be born into the family of David, and Micah is the first to tell us exactly where that would be. The ruler born in Bethlehem would be Jesus, the King over all the earth, and His kingdom would never end.

Some people may want to skip over a few chapters in the Old Testament. The books from the prophets seem like they are filled with harsh messages that can be hard to understand. But some exciting verses are tucked in between the warnings to God's people, and to-day's Bible verse is one of them!

TALK TO GOD
Thank God that you can learn many great things by reading every chapter of the Bible.

EXPLORE MORE: What does Micah 5:4 tell us about Jesus?

DID YOU KNOW?
The name Bethlehem means "house of bread," and Jesus calls himself the Bread of Life.

The Messiah would be born in Bethlehem.

The King Is Coming

Rejoice, people of Jerusalem. Shout for joy, people of Jerusalem. Your king is coming to you. He does what is right, and he saves. He is gentle and riding on a donkey. He is on the colt of a donkey. —Zechariah 9:9 ICB

The book of Zechariah is another book in the Old Testament where we can read future prophecies about Jesus. If you've ever celebrated Palm Sunday, you've probably heard the story of Jesus riding on a donkey into Jerusalem while people waved palm branches and shouted, "Hosanna!" But did you know Zechariah said that was going to happen more than five hundred years before Jesus was born? Zechariah even told the people to shout for joy when they saw their King riding on a donkey. Isn't that amazing?

TALK TO GOD
Thank God that His words are always true and that Jesus is coming back someday.

In today's verse, Zechariah told the Israelites what Jesus the Messiah would be like. He said Jesus would be their King, and He would be the one who will rule forever. Jesus would always do what is right. Jesus would also be their Savior and take away their sins. And Jesus would be gentle and humble—that's why He would ride on a donkey, which was a lowly animal and symbol of peace.

When we read the New Testament, we see that everything Zechariah said about Jesus was true. And what's even more wonderful is that Jesus, our King, is coming again! He will still do what is right. He will continue to be our Savior, and He will bring peace to the whole world. But this time, He will create His kingdom that will last forever. We know it's going to happen because God tells us in the Bible that it will, just like He told the prophet Zechariah many, many years ago. And when the King comes back, we can shout for joy just like the Israelites.

EXPLORE MORE: When Jesus comes back, what animal will He ride? Read Revelation 19:11 to find out.

Jesus is the King who is coming.

DID YOU KNOW?
A colt is a young male donkey that is less than four years old. A young female donkey less than four years old is called a filly.

Jesus's Special Family

This is the written story of the family line of Jesus the Messiah. He is the son of David. He is also the son of Abraham. —Matthew 1:1 NIrV

As we've been going through the stories of the Old Testament, we've seen how Jesus is everywhere in the Bible! Today is a special day because we get to start the New Testament. We will begin learning about what Jesus did when He lived on earth and how His disciples started the church after He went back to heaven. There are four books of the Bible that tell us all about Jesus's life. Those books are called *the Gospels*. They are the books of Matthew, Mark, Luke, and John.

Matthew was a tax collector before he became one of Jesus's twelve disciples. His gospel starts with the family line of Jesus. From the very beginning, Matthew calls Jesus the Messiah, which means He was the Savior God promised to send. Then Matthew tells us that Jesus was the Son of David and the Son of Abraham, which means He was a part of their families. Because Jesus was the Son of David, it means He came from the family of kings in the Old Testament. It also means He fulfilled the prophecy that the Messiah would be a part of David's family.

Matthew also connects Jesus to Abraham, which shows how God kept His promise to Abraham that everyone would be blessed through him. David and Abraham were two of the most important men in the Israelites' history. Since Jesus was a part of their family, it showed how important He was.

Jesus's family was perfectly planned by God. From the beginning, He knew exactly how He would accomplish His plan to send Jesus into the world. God always finishes what He starts.

EXPLORE MORE: Who are the two women mentioned in Jesus's family line in Matthew 1:5?

TALK TO GOD
Thank God for the perfect way He planned Jesus's family and birth, and for keeping all His promises.

DID YOU KNOW?
There were fourteen generations from Abraham to David, fourteen generations from David until the Israelites went to Babylon, and fourteen generations from that time until Jesus was born.

God planned Jesus's birth from the beginning.

Mary Trusts God's Plan

"You will become pregnant and give birth to a son. You must call him Jesus. He will be great and will be called the Son of the Most High God." —Luke 1:31–32 NIrV

The angel Gabriel had a lot of important announcements to make. Shortly after telling Zechariah that Elizabeth would have a baby, Gabriel visited a young girl named Mary in the town of Nazareth. Mary was engaged to a man named Joseph, who was from King David's family line. When Gabriel greeted Mary he said, "The Lord has blessed you in a special way. He is with you" (Luke 1:28). Mary was upset by what the angel said because she didn't understand what he meant. But Gabriel said, "Do not be afraid, Mary. God is very pleased with you. You will become pregnant and give birth to a son. You must call him Jesus." Then Gabriel told Mary that her baby boy would be the Son of God and would rule forever.

Mary didn't understand how she could have a baby when she wasn't married yet. Gabriel explained, "The Holy Spirit will come to you. The power of the Most High God will cover you." Gabriel told Mary that Elizabeth, her cousin, was having a baby even in her old age. "What God says always comes true," Gabriel said.

Mary replied, "I serve the Lord. May it happen to me just as you said it would."

TALK TO GOD
Tell God that you are willing to obey His plans for you.

Even though Mary didn't understand God's plans for her right away, she trusted that His plans were good. She did what God told her to do because she loved Him. There may be times when we don't understand the plans God has for us too. But we can remember that God loves us and wants what's best for us. And we can serve God with a willing heart just like Mary did.

EXPLORE MORE: Which prophecy about the Messiah was fulfilled through Mary? Read Isaiah 7:14 to find out.

I can obey God even when I don't understand.

DID YOU KNOW?
Nazareth is a town in the region of Galilee. Around the time Jesus was born, Nazareth was very small. Some people estimate that it had fewer than 500 people. Today more than 77,000 people live in Nazareth.

Joseph Listens to God

While Joseph thought about this, an angel of the Lord came to him in a dream. The angel said, "Joseph, descendant of David, don't be afraid to take Mary as your wife. The baby in her is from the Holy Spirit." —Matthew 1:20 ICB

Mary was engaged to marry a man named Joseph. The news of Mary's special baby must have been a big shock to Joseph since he and Mary weren't married yet. He must have had a lot of concerns and questions, and it was probably hard for him to understand what Mary told him about the angel's message.

The Bible says that Joseph was a good man and wanted to protect Mary. He decided not to marry her since he thought that was the right thing to do. He planned on breaking their engagement quietly. But then an angel visited Joseph in a dream. The angel said, "Don't be afraid to take Mary as your wife. The baby in her is from the Holy Spirit." The angel explained to Joseph God's wonderful and amazing plan. "You will name the son Jesus. Give him that name because he will save his people from their sins."

TALK TO GOD
Ask God to show you the right thing to do with a hard situation in your life.

When Joseph woke up, he did what the angel said and agreed to become Mary's husband. He followed God's plan and did what was right, even if it was very hard to understand.

Sometimes it can be hard to know the right thing to do. There isn't always a clear right or wrong way. But when we don't know what to do, we need to listen to what God says—by reading the Bible and talking to Him in prayer. Even though other people might have good advice, what God wants us to do is the most important thing. He always wants us to come to Him when we don't know what to do.

DID YOU KNOW?
Joseph was a carpenter, which means he built things. In Matthew 13, some people called Jesus "the son of the carpenter."

EXPLORE MORE: What can we do to find God's path? Look up Proverbs 3:5-6 to find out.

God tells me the right thing to do.

God with Us

"The virgin is going to have a baby. She will give birth to a son. And he will be called Immanuel." The name Immanuel means "God with us." —Matthew 1:23 NIrV

Have you ever heard people call Jesus "Immanuel"? We often hear this name for Jesus around Christmastime. You may have heard the Christmas song, "O Come, O Come Emmanuel." This name can be spelled with an *I*, from the Hebrew version, or an *E* from the Greek version. But do you know why Jesus is called "Immanuel"?

Matthew 1:23 tells us the name Immanuel means "God with us." It means that when Jesus was born, He was God in a human body, right here on earth, living with His people. And what's really special about this name is that the prophet Isaiah told us Jesus would be called Immanuel hundreds of years before He was born.

Isaiah said, "The Lord himself will give you a sign. The virgin is going to have a baby. She will give birth to a son. And he will be called Immanuel" (Isaiah 7:14). Matthew tells us everything that happened with Mary and Joseph, and the birth of Jesus fulfilled what God said in Isaiah. How wonderful is that!

TALK TO GOD
Tell Jesus how thankful you are that He came down to earth and lived a life just like you.

Even though Jesus isn't living on earth today, He is still God with us. He understands exactly how we feel and what it's like to be us because He lived a human life. He didn't just try to help us from far away, He came down to where we live and became one of us so He could save us. He is always with us through the Holy Spirit in our hearts. He is always listening when we need someone to talk to. And one day we will see Him face to face and live with Him forever. Jesus truly is Immanuel!

EXPLORE MORE: Read Hebrews 4:14–16. According to these verses, how was Jesus like us?

DID YOU KNOW?
The song "O Come, O Come Emmanuel" comes from a poem written in the eighth century. It was translated into English by J. M. Neale in 1851.

Jesus is God with us.

Jesus Is Born

While Joseph and Mary were there, the time came for the child to be born. —Luke 2:6 NIrV

Caesar Augustus was the first emperor of Rome. He wanted to count the people in the whole Roman empire. He ordered everyone to go to their family's hometown to be counted in a census. Since Joseph was from David's family, he had to travel to Bethlehem with Mary, who would soon be having a baby. It may have taken five or six days for them to travel from Nazareth to Bethlehem, and it was not an easy trip! The winding mountain trails were dusty and bumpy, and some were not very safe.

When they finally reached Bethlehem, the small town was crowded with many travelers who had come for the census. While they were there, the time came for Jesus to be born. Mary wrapped Him in strips of cloth and placed Him in a manger because there was no room for them in the inn.

We don't know for sure where Joseph and Mary stayed. It might have been a stable, or maybe an open space on the bottom floor of a house where families kept their animals. What we do know is that Jesus left His beautiful home in heaven so He could come to earth to save us. He was born to be a King, but His first bed was a manger—a stone box that was used for feeding animals.

Jesus, the Messiah, was born in Bethlehem, just like the prophet Micah had foretold nearly seven hundred years earlier. This story shows us again how the Old Testament and New Testament fit together and how God makes all His words come true.

EXPLORE MORE: Read John 18:37. What is the reason Jesus gave for being born?

TALK TO GOD
Thank God for sending Jesus into the world so He could be our Lord and Savior.

DID YOU KNOW?
It's about 70 miles (112 kilometers) from Nazareth to Bethlehem. The road is often referred to as the Nativity Trail.

God planned that Jesus would be born in Bethlehem.

Shepherds and Angels

Today in the town of David a Savior has been born to you.
He is the Messiah, the Lord. —Luke 2:11 NIrV

On the night Jesus was born, some shepherds were watching their sheep in a field near Bethlehem. This was something they did every night, but this night was different from all the other nights. While the shepherds were caring for their sheep, a bright angel suddenly appeared. The shepherds were terrified! But the angel said, "Do not be afraid. I bring you good news. It will bring great joy for all the people" (Luke 2:10).

TALK TO GOD
Thank God for the gift of Jesus. Ask Him to help you share the good news with others.

The good news was that the Messiah had been born! The angel told the shepherds to go to Bethlehem and they would find the baby wrapped in strips of cloth and lying in a manger. Then an army of angels filled the sky, praising God and saying, "May glory be given to God in the highest heaven! And may peace be given to those He is pleased with on earth."

When the angels went back to heaven, the shepherds said, "Let's go to Bethlehem. Let's see this thing that has happened, which the Lord has told us about." So, they hurried to Bethlehem and found the baby lying in the manger. Everything was just like the angel had said it would be.

Some people wonder why God sent the angel to share the news of Jesus's birth with shepherds instead of an important king or ruler. During Bible times, people looked down on shepherds. They were often dirty and smelly from living out in the fields. But Jesus came to earth to save everyone who believed in Him—from royal kings to lowly shepherds. God loves everyone and wants all people to believe in Jesus.

EXPLORE MORE: Read Luke 2:17–20. What did the shepherds do after they saw Jesus? What did Mary do?

Jesus came for everyone.

DID YOU KNOW?
Lambs that were brought to the temple for sacrifice were often wrapped in strips of cloth. When the shepherds saw Jesus wrapped in strips of cloth, they were looking at the Lamb of God, who would sacrifice himself for us.

Three Dreams

After they left, an angel of the Lord came to Joseph in a dream. The angel said, "Get up! Take the child and his mother and escape to Egypt." —Matthew 2:13 ICB

Herod was upset when the wise men left Jerusalem without coming to see him. He wanted to find Jesus, too, but it wasn't so he could worship Him. Herod was a mean and jealous king who wanted to kill Jesus.

An angel of the Lord warned Joseph in a dream to take Mary and Jesus to Egypt where they would be safe. Joseph listened to God. He got up in the middle of the night and traveled with Mary and Jesus to Egypt. They lived there until Herod died.

Then Joseph had another dream. This time the angel of the Lord told him they could go back to Israel. So, Joseph brought Mary and Jesus home to Israel. When Joseph heard that Herod's son was the new king of Judea, he was afraid to go to Bethlehem. Joseph was warned in a third dream and took Mary and Jesus to live in Nazareth, a town in Galilee.

TALK TO GOD
Thank God that we can learn so much about Jesus by reading the Bible.

The dreams God gave Joseph kept Jesus safe from an evil king, but that's not the only reason God sent them. When Joseph left Egypt with Mary and Jesus, it fulfilled what God had said through Hosea the prophet. Hosea 11:1 says, "When Israel was a child, I loved him. And I called my son out of Egypt." And in Matthew 2:23 it says, "What God had said through the prophets came true: 'He will be called a Nazarene.'" Jesus grew up in Nazareth and many people called Him "Jesus of Nazareth."

God gave the prophets messages to help people know that Jesus was the Messiah. And He gave dreams to Joseph to make His messages come true.

EXPLORE MORE: Read John 1:45–46. What question did Nathaniel ask Jesus's disciple?

DID YOU KNOW?
Nazareth was a small town about 55 miles (88.5 kilometers) north of Jerusalem. The people from Nazareth were looked down upon by Judeans.

God's words always come true.

Jesus Amazes the Teachers

Everyone who heard him was amazed at how much he understood. They also were amazed at his answers. —Luke 2:47 NIrV

When Jesus was twelve years old, He went to Jerusalem with His parents to celebrate the Passover. The Jewish people celebrated this festival every year to remember how God delivered their ancestors from Egypt. Jesus and His family traveled for several days with many other people until they finally reached Jerusalem. The Passover lasted seven days. During that time, they ate special meals and offered sacrifices to God at the temple.

As Joseph and Mary traveled home, they thought Jesus was with their friends or relatives, but when they looked for Him, they couldn't find Him. They finally went back to the temple and found Jesus with the teachers of the law, listening and asking questions. The teachers were amazed at how much Jesus knew and understood. Joseph and Mary told Jesus they had been very worried. But Jesus said, "Why were you looking for me? Didn't you know I had to be in my Father's house?" (Luke 2:49). They didn't understand what Jesus meant, but Mary remembered what He said and kept it like a treasure in her heart.

TALK TO GOD
Ask Jesus to teach you with His great wisdom.

Jesus went back to Nazareth with His parents and obeyed them. This is the only Bible story about Jesus as a boy. But in Luke 2:52 ERV it says, "As Jesus grew taller, he continued to grow in wisdom. God was pleased with him and so were the people who knew him."

Jesus had to grow up, just like you do, and He understands what it's like to be a kid. Whenever you need to talk to Him, He will listen—just like He listened to the teachers at the temple.

EXPLORE MORE: How did the people respond to Jesus when He first began His ministry? Read Mark 1:21–22 to find out.

Jesus will listen to me.

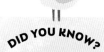

DID YOU KNOW?
From age six to age ten, a child can grow as much as ten inches.

A Preacher in the Desert

When it was the right time, John the Baptizer began telling people
a message from God. This was out in the desert area of Judea.
—Matthew 3:1 ERV

Mary's relative Elizabeth had a baby boy a few months before Jesus was born. His name was John, and God had important work for him to do. God chose John to prepare the way for Jesus's ministry on earth. He lived in the desert and ate locusts and wild honey. He wore clothes made from camel's hair and tied a leather belt around his waist.

John was a preacher in the desert of Judea. Many people from all over Judea came to see him. His message was, "Change your hearts and lives, because God's kingdom is now very near" (Matthew 3:2). When the people said they were sorry for their sins, John baptized them in the Jordan River.

TALK TO GOD
Ask God to help you
do important things
for Him.

The prophet Isaiah had prophesied about John. In Isaiah 40:3 it says, "Listen, there is someone shouting: 'Prepare a way in the desert for the Lord. Make a straight road there for our God.'"

John told his followers that someone greater and more powerful was coming soon. John was talking about Jesus. John said that he baptized with water, but Jesus would baptize with the Holy Spirit.

Even though many people followed John the Baptist, he never thought he was important. In verses 28 and 30 of John chapter 3, he said, "'I am not the Messiah. I am only the one God sent to prepare the way for him. . . . He must become more and more important, and I must become less important."

Many people have important jobs, and we all have important things to do. But no one is more important than Jesus, and nothing is more important than telling others about Him.

EXPLORE MORE: Read what John said about Jesus in Mark 1:7.

DID YOU KNOW?

Locusts belong to the grasshopper family, and people in many countries eat them. They are packed with protein and can be smoked, fried, or roasted until they are crunchy.

Jesus is more important than anyone.

Jesus Is Baptized

A voice from heaven said, "This is my Son, and I love him. I am very pleased with him." —Matthew 3:17 NIrV

One day Jesus came from Galilee and saw John the Baptist at the Jordan River. Jesus asked John to baptize Him. At first John was confused and said that Jesus should baptize him instead. But Jesus said, "Let it be this way for now. It is right for us to do this. It carries out God's holy plan." So John agreed to baptize Jesus.

When Jesus came up out of the water, the heavens opened, and God's Spirit came down in the form of a dove and rested on Him. Then a voice from heaven said, "This is my Son, and I love him. I am very pleased with him."

The voice from heaven was the voice of God. He sent Jesus to earth to save the world from sin and show us how much God loves us. And Jesus also came to earth to teach people how to love God and how to love each other.

TALK TO GOD
Ask God to help you follow His plan for your life like Jesus did.

John baptized people after they turned away from their sin. Their baptism was a sign that they were choosing to follow God and have their sins washed away. Even though Jesus never sinned, He was baptized to show that He was obedient to following God's plan for His life on earth.

Jesus is our greatest example of how to live. Like Jesus, we can choose to follow God's plan for our lives and be obedient to Him. Even though we will never be able to live a life without sin, we can have our sins washed away by believing in Jesus. Jesus lived a perfect life for us, so we don't have to.

EXPLORE MORE: What did John say about Jesus in John 1:14–15?

Believing in Jesus washes my sins away.

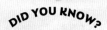

DID YOU KNOW?
Nearly a million visitors every year go to see where John baptized Jesus in the Jordan River, and many choose to get baptized there too.

Jesus Is Tempted

Jesus said to the devil, "Go away from me, Satan! It is written in the
Scriptures, 'You must worship the Lord your God. Serve only him!'"
—Matthew 4:10 ICB

After Jesus was baptized, the Holy Spirit led Him into the wilderness to be alone.
He didn't eat for forty days and was very hungry. The devil, who is also called Satan,
is God's enemy. He came to Jesus to make Him sin. First, he told Jesus to turn stones
into bread. But Jesus spoke the words from Deuteronomy 8:3. "It is written in the
Scriptures, 'A person does not live
only by eating bread. But a person lives by everything the
Lord says'" (Matthew 4:4).

Then Satan led Jesus
to a high place on the
temple and told Jesus to
jump off. He said God's
angels would catch Him.
But Jesus answered with
words from Deuteronomy
6:16, "Do not test the Lord
your God."

Satan tried one more time.
He took Jesus to a high mountain
and showed Him all the kingdoms of the world. He said,
"If you will bow down and worship me, I will give you all
these things." Jesus said to him, "Go away from me, Satan! It is
written in the Scriptures, 'You must worship the Lord your God. Serve only
him!'" Then Satan went away, and angels came to be with Jesus.

The devil tempted Jesus because he wanted Jesus to sin against God. But Jesus
didn't listen to him. Jesus spoke words from Scripture to help Him stay strong against
temptation. Satan wants us to sin too, and Jesus is our example of what to do when
we're tempted. You can think about Bible verses you know. You can remember that
obeying God is always right. And you can ask God to help you be strong. Temptation
can be strong, but God is stronger.

TALK TO GOD
Ask God to help you
be strong when you
are tempted.

EXPLORE MORE: What does 1 Corinthians 10:13 say about
temptation?

DID YOU KNOW?
The highest point
of the temple was
called the pinnacle,
and it was located
at the southeast
corner of the
building.

Jesus is my example of how to
face temptation.

Jesus Goes to Capernaum

[Jesus] left Nazareth and went and lived in Capernaum, a town near Lake Galilee. Capernaum is in the area near Zebulun and Naphtali.
—Matthew 4:13 ICB

We know from reading the Bible that Jesus moved from one place to another. He was born in Bethlehem, and then lived in Egypt where God kept Him safe from King Herod. After that, Jesus grew up in Nazareth in the region of Galilee. All these places fulfilled what the Old Testament prophets said about the Messiah.

In Matthew 4, we learn that Jesus left Nazareth and began His teaching ministry in Capernaum, in the area of Zebulun and Naphtali by the Sea of Galilee. And do you know what? This fulfilled an Old Testament prophecy too!

TALK TO GOD
Thank God for all the verses in the Bible that point to Jesus.

In Isaiah 9, the prophet Isaiah said the land of Zebulun and Naphtali would be made great. This land stretched along the Mediterranean Sea to the land along the Jordan River. It continued north to Galilee where the people who were not Israelites lived. Isaiah 9:2 says, "Now those people live in darkness. But they will see a great light. They live in a place that is very dark. But a light will shine on them." That light is Jesus.

God sent Jesus to be a light to the world—to the Jewish people and also to people who are not Jewish, called gentiles. Most of His time was spent in the region of Galilee, but news about Jesus spread all over the world.

The prophets of the Old Testament and disciples of the New Testament wrote down the words God gave them. Because they did, the whole world can know that Jesus is the Son of God who came to save us. He is a light in the darkness to shine for all to see.

EXPLORE MORE: According to Isaiah 9:3, what would happen to the people living in Zebulun and Naphtali?

Jesus is a light in the darkness.

DID YOU KNOW?
Zebulun and Naphtali were two of Jacob's sons. Their descendants became two of the tribes that settled in the northern area of the promised land.

Jesus Finds His First Followers

"Come and follow me," Jesus said. "I will send you out to fish for people." —Matthew 4:19 NIrV

As Jesus walked along the Sea of Galilee, He saw two fishermen throwing nets into the water. One was Simon, who was also called Peter, and the other was his brother, Andrew. Jesus called to them, "Come and follow me! I will send you out to fish for people." Do you know what Simon and Andrew did? They left their nets right there and followed Jesus.

Farther along the shore, Jesus saw two more fishermen who were also brothers. Their names were James and John, and they were fixing their nets with their father, Zebedee. Jesus said, "Come and follow me!" Do you know what they did? They left everything and followed Jesus!

A man named Philip also agreed to follow Jesus. Then Philip told his friend Nathanael about Jesus. He said, "We have found the one whom Moses wrote about in the Law. The prophets also wrote about him. He is Jesus of Nazareth, the son of Joseph."

At first, Nathanael doubted. "Can anything good come from Nazareth?" he asked.

But when Jesus saw Nathanael, He said, "He is a true Israelite. Nothing about him is false."

Nathanael was surprised. "How do you know me?" he asked. Jesus said, "I saw you under the fig tree, before Philip told you about me." Then Nathanael knew Jesus was the Son of God, and he followed Jesus too.

These men learned from John the Baptist that the Messiah was coming soon. They also knew what the Old Testament prophets had written. Their hearts were ready to meet Jesus and follow Him. When people's hearts are ready to follow Jesus, they will know and believe that He is the Messiah.

TALK TO GOD
Ask God to help you follow Jesus every day.

DID YOU KNOW?
In Bible times, fishing with nets was usually done at night so the fish couldn't see the nets. Otherwise they would swim around the nets and not get caught.

EXPLORE MORE: Read Mark 3:17 to find out the name Jesus gave to James and John.

My heart is ready to follow Jesus.

Jesus's First Miracle

This was the first of all the miraculous signs Jesus did. He did it in the town of Cana in Galilee. By this he showed his divine greatness, and his followers believed in him. —John 2:11 ERV

Jesus was invited to a wedding in Cana, which was in Galilee. He went with His mother, Mary, and some of His followers. In Bible times weddings were big celebrations and lasted for several days. Jesus's mother came to Him and said, "They have no more wine."

Mary must have known that Jesus could help. He hadn't done any miracles yet, but she knew that God's power was in Him. Maybe she remembered the words the angel Gabriel had said—that Jesus would be great and would be the Son of the Most High. Maybe she remembered the words of Simeon who said, "I have seen with my own eyes how God will save His people." Mary treasured many things in her heart, so somehow, she knew Jesus could help. Mary said to the wedding servants, "Do whatever He tells you to do."

TALK TO GOD
Say thank you to Jesus that He has power to do miracles.

Jesus saw six stone water jars that the Jewish people used for their washing ceremonies. He told the servants to fill them with water, so they did. Then Jesus said, "Dip out some water and take it to the man in charge of the feast."

When the man in charge tasted the water, it had turned into wine. He didn't know where the new wine came from, but the servants and Jesus's followers knew. The man said to the bridegroom, "People serve the best wine first, but you have saved the best for now."

That was the first miracle Jesus did on earth to show He was the Son of God. His followers were amazed and put their faith in Him. And they would continue to be amazed as they kept following Him.

EXPLORE MORE: Read Acts 2:22 to see what Peter said about Jesus.

Jesus's power is amazing.

DID YOU KNOW?
The Wedding Feast at Cana is a famous oil painting by Paolo Veronese painted in 1563. Until 1700, the painting hung in the San Giorgio Monastery in Venice, Italy. It now hangs in the Louvre Museum in Paris, France.

Jesus Shows His Power

The people were amazed. They asked each other, "What is happening here? This man is teaching something new. And he teaches with authority. He even gives commands to evil spirits, and they obey him." —Mark 1:27 ICB

Jesus was in Capernaum on the Sabbath day. He went into the synagogue, which is like a temple, and began to teach. The people who listened to Him were amazed that Jesus spoke with more authority than the teachers of the law.

While Jesus was teaching, a man came into the synagogue who had an evil spirit in him. The evil spirit cried out, "Jesus of Nazareth! What do you want with us? Did you come to destroy us? I know who you are—God's Holy One!" (Mark 1:24).

Then Jesus commanded, "Be quiet! Come out of the man!" The man began to shake, and the spirit gave a loud cry and came out of him.

The people were stunned. They saw with their own eyes and heard with their own ears everything that happened. They said, "What is happening? Even the evil spirits obey Him!"

This miracle showed that Jesus has power over Satan. No power in heaven or earth is greater than God's power. And since Jesus is the Son of God, He has God's power within Him.

TALK TO GOD
Thank Jesus that He cares about people and can help them.

The news about Jesus spread quickly through Galilee. Many more people began following Jesus to listen to Him teach and watch His miracles. People who were sick came to Jesus to be healed, and many believed in Him.

You can follow Jesus too by reading these amazing stories in your Bible and learning more about His earthly ministry. You can ask Jesus to help you with any problems you have. And you can thank Him that He cares for you just like He cared for people long ago.

EXPLORE MORE: Who did Jesus heal in Mark 1:29–31?

DID YOU KNOW?

A synagogue is a place of worship for Jewish people. It is believed that synagogues were first used by the Israelites when they were in Babylon.

Jesus's power is the greatest of all.

Jesus Heals a Humble Man

Jesus reached out his hand and touched the man. "I am willing to do it," he said. "Be 'clean'!" —Luke 5:13 NIrV

Jesus was walking through a town when a man with a bad skin disease came to Him. The man fell face down to the ground when he saw Jesus. The man begged Jesus, "Lord, if you are willing to make me 'clean,' you can do it."

Jesus had compassion for the man. He reached out His hand and touched the man. "I am willing to do it," he said. "Be 'clean'!" And just like that, the man was completely healed of His skin disease.

TALK TO GOD
Thank Jesus that He has the power to heal.

The man's skin disease was called leprosy, and it was common in Jesus's day. One person could catch it easily from someone who had it, and it was very serious. People who had it needed to live by themselves or with other lepers. If people with leprosy went out to be around other people, they would shout, "Unclean, unclean," to warn others to stay away from them.

The man with leprosy must have heard about Jesus's miracles and how He could heal people. He believed that Jesus could make him well, so he went out to find Him. The way he talked to Jesus showed that he was a humble man. He didn't demand that Jesus heal him. He said, "Lord, if you are willing."

Jesus reached out and touched the man to heal him. This was not something anyone else would have done. People were afraid to get close to someone with leprosy because they didn't want to get the disease. By touching the man, Jesus showed His love. By healing the man, Jesus showed His power. The news about Jesus continued to spread, and crowds of people followed Jesus wherever He went.

EXPLORE MORE: What did Jesus tell the man to do after He healed his skin disease? Luke 5:14 will give you the answer.

DID YOU KNOW?
Leprosy is also known as Hansen's disease. It can now be cured with a combination of antibiotics. The World Health Organization provides free treatment for people with leprosy.

Jesus is willing to heal people.

Matthew Follows Jesus

Jesus heard the Pharisees ask this. So he said, "Healthy people don't need a doctor. Only the sick need a doctor." —Matthew 9:12 ICB

As Jesus walked through the town of Capernaum, he saw a man named Matthew, who was also called Levi. Matthew was sitting in a booth where he collected taxes from the Jewish people. Even though Matthew was Jewish, he worked for the Roman government.

The Jewish people did not like tax collectors. The Roman leaders asked for too much money from the Jews, and many of the tax collectors were not honest. Sometimes they would take extra money from the people and keep it for themselves.

Jesus looked at Matthew in his booth. "Follow me," He said. So Matthew left his booth and followed Jesus.

Matthew invited Jesus to his house for dinner. He invited other people too, including more tax collectors. When the Pharisees saw Jesus at Matthew's house, they asked His disciples, "Why does your teacher eat with tax collectors and 'sinners'?"

When Jesus heard what they said He replied, "Healthy people don't need a doctor. Only the sick need a doctor." Then He told them to learn what this means: "I want faithful love more than I want animal sacrifices." Those are words from the prophet Hosea (Hosea 6:6).

Jesus wants all people to follow Him, no matter how good or bad they seem. He wants to give us a new life that only He can give. But Jesus wants people to follow Him because they love Him. He doesn't care about traditions and sacrifices and offerings if people's hearts are not right with God.

Jesus reached out to sinful people because they needed a Savior. And He still reaches out to people today—because everyone still needs a Savior.

EXPLORE MORE: Read Mark 3:16–19 to learn the names of the twelve disciples who followed Jesus.

TALK TO GOD
Thank Jesus that He invites everyone to follow Him.

DID YOU KNOW?
The book of Matthew includes nine references to Old Testament prophecies that Jesus fulfilled. Matthew refers to more verses from the Old Testament than any other New Testament book.

Jesus wants all people to follow Him.

Jesus and Nicodemus

God so loved the world that he gave his one and only Son. Anyone who believes in him will not die but will have eternal life. —John 3:16 NIrV

Nicodemus was an important Jewish ruler who wanted to talk to Jesus, so he met with Jesus at night. Maybe he didn't want other Jewish rulers to see him talking to Jesus. They didn't want anything to do with Jesus, but Nicodemus knew there was something special about Him. Nicodemus had seen Jesus heal people. He said to Jesus, "We know that God is with you. If he weren't, you couldn't do the signs you are doing."

Jesus told Nicodemus, "What I'm about to tell you is true. No one can see God's kingdom unless they are born again."

Nicodemus was confused. He didn't understand how someone can be born a second time. But Jesus wasn't talking about being born again as a baby. Jesus meant that by believing in Him, people can have a new life on earth and a home in heaven that lasts forever. It's a person's spirit that gets born again, not their body.

TALK TO GOD
Thank God for sending Jesus to die on the cross so that everyone who believes in Him can have eternal life, including you!

Today's Bible verse, John 3:16, is like putting the whole message of the Bible into one verse. God sent Jesus to earth because He loves us so much and wants us to live with Him forever. God is holy, and we are not. That's why God sent His Son to die on the cross to pay for our sins, so we can be made holy. God didn't send Jesus to earth to tell us how bad we are. God sent Jesus to save us.

Being born again is not about obeying rules. It's believing that Jesus is the Son of God and asking Him to be our Savior. Then we can follow Jesus and love Him back.

EXPLORE MORE: Read John 19:38–40 to find out something Nicodemus did after Jesus died.

DID YOU KNOW?
For a football game in 2009, Tim Tebow wrote John 3:16 in black under his eye. That day, 90 million people googled the Bible verse to see what it says.

God sent Jesus because He loves me.

Salty and Bright

"You are the light that shines for the world to see. You are like a city built on a hill that cannot be hidden." —Matthew 5:14 ERV

After Jesus finished preaching the Beatitudes, He taught His followers another lesson. Jesus said they were like salt and light. It might sound strange, but those were two important things during Bible times.

First Jesus said, "You are the salt of the earth. But suppose the salt loses its saltiness. How can it be made salty again? It is no longer good for anything." During the time Jesus lived, salt was worth a lot of money. Jesus was saying His followers are precious to God. Salt was also used to add flavor and keep meat from going bad. Jesus wanted His followers to bring flavor to the world through their joy. He wanted them to keep themselves and the world from "going bad" by guarding against sin.

Next Jesus said, "You are the light that shines for the world to see. . . . People don't hide a lamp under a bowl. They put it on a lampstand. Then the light shines for everyone in the house." We don't turn on a light and hide it. In the same way, Jesus wanted His followers to be a light for other people. He wanted them to live so others would see the good things they did and praise God.

TALK TO GOD
Ask God to help you shine brightly for Him and to add His flavor wherever you go.

Even though Jesus spoke these words thousands of years ago, He still wants His followers to be salt and light. We are precious to God, and we can give people a taste of what God is like by loving them the way He does. Jesus is like a bright light that shines into our hearts. We can shine His light by caring for others and showing the love and peace of Jesus. We can be salty and bright!

EXPLORE MORE: What did Jesus say about himself in John 8:12?

DID YOU KNOW?
Salt used to be so valuable that it was used as money for trade. This is where the phrase "worth his salt" comes from.

I am salt and light.

Teach Us to Pray

One day Jesus was praying in a certain place. When he finished, one of his disciples spoke to him. "Lord," he said, "teach us to pray, just as John taught his disciples." —Luke 11:1 NIrV

Jesus often went to quiet places to pray. Sometimes He went by himself, and sometimes His disciples went with Him. One day when He was praying, one of His disciples said, "Lord, teach us to pray."

Jesus said, "When you pray, this is what you should say. 'Father, may your name be honored. May your kingdom come. Give us each day our daily bread. Forgive us our sins, as we also forgive everyone who sins against us. Keep us from falling into sin when we are tempted.'"

TALK TO GOD
Pray the words of the Lord's Prayer found in Matthew 6:9–13.

This special prayer became known as the Lord's Prayer, and many Christians have learned it over the years. Groups of Christians will often say this prayer at church or other special services. Have you ever heard these words before? Whether or not you know this prayer, you can pray the way Jesus taught His disciples. You can start by telling God how wonderful His name is and ask that it be treated as holy. Then you can ask God to bring His kingdom to earth—by having His way each day and having Jesus return to build His kingdom.

Next you can ask God for what you need today. Nothing is too big or small to ask for. Then, ask God to forgive your sins and help you forgive others when they do something wrong to you. Finally, you can end your prayer by asking God to keep you from doing the wrong thing when you are tempted.

The Lord's Prayer is a great way to pray, and there are many other ways to pray too. Any time we pray with an open heart, God will listen to us.

EXPLORE MORE: Read Romans 8:26–27. What does the Holy Spirit do for us when we don't know what to pray?

Jesus teaches us how to pray.

DID YOU KNOW?
Other names for the Lord's Prayer are the Our Father, Oratio Dominica (which means "Lord's Prayer" in Latin), and the Pater Noster (which means "Our Father" in Latin).

Don't Worry

"The thing you should want most is God's kingdom and doing what God wants. Then all these other things you need will be given to you." —Matthew 6:33 ICB

Have you ever seen a bird going shopping at the grocery store? Or have you ever seen a flower making a beautiful dress to wear? Of course not! That would be so silly! Birds find their food outside each day as they fly around. And flowers don't need to create fancy clothes because their petals are so beautiful. God gives the birds what they need to eat each day, and God makes the flowers of the fields look more beautiful than the fanciest dress.

That's exactly what Jesus taught His followers on the mountainside. He said that when we see birds, we can remember God feeds them every day. And when we look at flowers growing in a field, we can remember God dresses them in beautiful colors. Jesus told the people that God would take care of them too: "And you know that you are worth much more than the birds," He said. "God clothes the grass in the field . . . so you can be even more sure that God will clothe you."

Jesus wants us to know God will always give us what we need, just like He told His followers long ago. Instead of worrying about what to eat or what to wear, Jesus wants us to spend our time thinking about God's kingdom and what God wants us to do. God already knows what we need and how He will give it to us. Whether we have a lot or a little, He promises to always watch over us, so we can think about more important things like loving and serving Him.

EXPLORE MORE: Jesus said the flowers were dressed fancier than one of the richest kings in history. Read Matthew 6:29 to find out who it was.

TALK TO GOD
Ask God to give you what you need today and thank Him for always taking care of you.

DID YOU KNOW?
The type of food birds eat depends on their species and the time of year. During the spring and summer, songbirds eat insects and spiders. In the winter, birds that don't migrate eat fruit and seeds.

God gives me what I need.

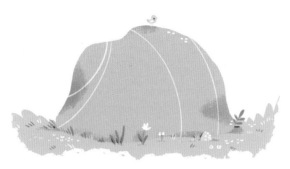

Solid Rock

"Anyone who listens to my teaching and follows it is wise, like a person who builds a house on solid rock." —Matthew 7:24 NLT

When construction workers start building a house, one of the first things they do is make a foundation. The foundation is usually something hard and sturdy—like concrete or stone. It's like a base that the rest of the house is built on. The job of a foundation is to hold up the weight of the house and keep water and wet soil from getting in. The foundation is the most important part of the house.

TALK TO GOD
Ask God to help you build your life on Jesus.

Jesus told His followers that we all have the choice to build on a good foundation. But He wasn't talking about building a house. He was talking about following His teaching in our lives. When we hear Jesus's words and do what He says, we become like a wise person who builds a house on solid rock. When bad things happen, Jesus told us we will be like a strong house in a big storm: "Though the rain comes in torrents and the floodwaters rise and the winds beat against that house, it won't collapse because it is built on bedrock."

Jesus also told us what happens when people hear His words and don't follow Him. He said, "But anyone who hears my teaching and doesn't obey it is foolish, like a person who builds a house on sand. When the rains and floods come and the winds beat against that house, it will collapse with a mighty crash."

What we choose to build our lives on is the most important decision we make. We can choose to build our lives on doing things our own way like sinking sand, or the solid rock of Jesus's perfect teaching.

EXPLORE MORE: What is God called in Deuteronomy 32:4?

Jesus is the solid rock.

DID YOU KNOW?
Reinforced concrete is used to create foundations for many new houses. Builders make wooden forms and then put steel reinforcing bars in between the forms. The forms are filled with poured concrete to finish the foundation.

The Farmer and His Seeds

"Still other seed fell on good soil. It grew up and produced a crop 30, 60, or even 100 times more than the farmer planted."
—Mark 4:8 NIrV

As Jesus began teaching by the Sea of Galilee, people crowded around Him. So, Jesus sat in a boat and taught those who were on shore. Jesus told a parable, which is a story to help people understand the truth of God's Word.

Jesus said, "A farmer went out to plant seeds and scattered them on the ground. Some seeds fell on a hard path, but the birds came and ate them. Some seeds fell in rocky places where there wasn't enough soil. The plants grew quickly but dried up from the sun because they had no roots. Other seeds landed among thorns, which crowded out the plants when they started to grow. But the seeds that fell on good soil produced a crop of thirty, sixty, or one hundred times more than the farmer planted."

TALK TO GOD
Ask God to help you have a heart that's always open to learning more about Him.

When the disciples were alone with Jesus, they asked Him the meaning of the parable. Jesus explained that the seed is like God's message and the soil is like the hearts of people who hear it. Some people hear God's message but don't believe it because their hearts are like the hard path. Other people believe for a while but then turn away because their hearts are like the rocky soil. Some people love the things of the world, which are like thorns that keep them from loving God. But people who hear God's message and believe it are like the good soil. Their hearts are ready to follow Jesus and share God's message with others.

Today, people's hearts are still like that. Some believe God's message, and some don't. You can ask God to help your heart be like good soil so you can keep growing and loving Him.

EXPLORE MORE: Read John 1:12–13. What right do people have when they believe in Jesus?

DID YOU KNOW?
Bible teachers agree that there are close to forty parables of Jesus in the Gospels.

I want to keep learning and growing.

The Storm Obeys

Jesus stood up and gave a command to the wind and the water. He said, "Quiet! Be still!" Then the wind stopped, and the lake became calm. —Mark 4:39 ERV

One evening, after Jesus finished teaching a crowd, He asked His disciples to go with Him across the lake. They got into the boat and began to cross the lake when a strong wind came. The waves grew bigger until they splashed over the sides of the boat and started filling the bottom with water.

While all this happened, Jesus was sleeping. The disciples woke Him up. "Teacher," they said, "don't you care about us? We are going to drown!"

Jesus stood up and spoke to the wind and waves. "Quiet! Be still!" He said. The wind stopped, and the water in the lake became calm. He said to His disciples, "Why are you afraid? Do you still have no faith?"

The disciples were scared and asked each other, "What kind of man is this? Even the wind and the water obey him!"

TALK TO GOD
Thank Jesus that He is with you even when you feel afraid.

In the beginning of Genesis, we read that God created the sky and seas. The gospel of John tells us Jesus was with God at creation, and everything was created through Him. Jesus was not afraid of the storm because He knew creation would obey Him. But Jesus was surprised by the way His disciples acted. Jesus understood why the storm frightened them, but He was with them. They had everything they needed to get through the storm safely. He would protect them.

Sometimes we act like the disciples and forget that Jesus is always with us through the Holy Spirit in our hearts. No matter what scary things we face, Jesus promises He will never leave us. We don't have to be afraid because He is bigger than all our fears.

EXPLORE MORE: Read John 1:1–5 to see that Jesus (the Word) was with God at creation.

Jesus is in control.

DID YOU KNOW?
The lake Jesus and the disciples crossed was the Sea of Galilee. It is also known as Lake Tiberias and is the lowest freshwater lake on earth. It is about 686 feet (209 meters) below sea level.

The Best Healer of All

When Jesus went back to Galilee, the people welcomed him. Everyone was waiting for him. —Luke 8:40 ERV

As news about Jesus spread, many people came to Him to be healed. Some were blind, some couldn't walk, and some brought friends and family who were sick. A man name Jairus was a leader in Galilee. His daughter was very sick. Jairus begged Jesus to come to his house.

While Jesus was going with Jairus, a woman came behind Jesus hoping she wouldn't be seen. She had a sickness that made her bleed for twelve years. She spent all her money on doctors, but no one could heal her. She touched the bottom of Jesus's coat. Jesus said, "Who touched me?"

Peter answered, "Master, people are all around you, pushing against you."

Jesus replied, "Someone touched me. I felt power go out from me."

The woman bowed before Jesus. She said she was healed the moment she touched Jesus's coat.

Jesus said to her, "My daughter, you are made well because you believed. Go in peace." Just then someone came from Jairus's house and told him his daughter had died. Jesus told Jairus, "Don't be afraid! Just believe and your daughter will be well." Jesus went into the house with Peter, James, John, and the girl's parents. Jesus said, "Don't cry. She is not dead. She is only sleeping." Jesus took her hand and said, "Little girl, stand up!" Her spirit came back, and she stood up.

TALK TO GOD
Pray for someone you know who needs Jesus's healing.

Jesus has the power to make people well, and He has the power to raise people from the dead. One day He will heal all our sickness and hurts and give us a forever life with Him. We can have faith to believe just like the woman and Jairus.

EXPLORE MORE: Read Psalm 103:1–3. Why should we praise God?

DID YOU KNOW?
The woman who was bleeding was considered unclean by Jewish law. She tried to touch Jesus's robe in secret because she could have been punished for touching someone while she was sick.

Jesus is my healer.

Two Blind Men Have Faith

They went right into the house where he was staying, and Jesus asked them, "Do you believe I can make you see?" "Yes, Lord," they told him, "we do." —Matthew 9:28 NLT

After Jesus healed Jairus's daughter, two blind men followed Him. They shouted, "Son of David, have mercy on us!" They followed Jesus right into the house where He was staying.

He asked them, "Do you believe I can make you see?"

They answered, "Yes, Lord, we do." Jesus touched their eyes and said, "Because of your faith, it will happen." They could see immediately! Jesus warned them "Don't tell anyone about this." But they told people about Him all over the area.

After this, another man was brought to Jesus. He was being controlled by a demon and could not speak. Jesus commanded the demon to come out of the man, and then the man was able to talk. The crowds were amazed to see such a powerful thing happen. They said, "Nothing like this has ever happened in Israel!"

TALK TO GOD
Ask Jesus to help you believe in Him more each day.

Jesus loved all the people who came to Him for healing. It must have hurt His heart to see their sicknesses and disabilities. We know Jesus wanted them to get better because He healed them. But even more than that, Jesus cared about what they believed. He wanted them to be spiritually healthy too. That's why Jesus often pointed out people's faith or asked if they believed—like the woman who had been bleeding and the blind men who came into His house.

Jesus wants the same thing for us today. He wants us to love Him and believe in His power as the Son of God. We can always ask Jesus for what we need. His love is the greatest thing we can ever receive from Him.

EXPLORE MORE: What did Jesus do after these miracles? Read Matthew 9:35–38 to find out.

Jesus cares about our faith.

DID YOU KNOW?
There are at least eight stories in the Gospels where Jesus healed blind people. He healed them in different ways. Sometimes He spoke, one time He spit on a man's eyes, and another time He used clay.

Disciples on a Mission

"As you go, preach this message, 'The kingdom of heaven has come near.' Heal those who are sick. Bring those who are dead back to life. Make those who have skin diseases 'clean' again. Drive out demons. You have received freely, so give freely." —Matthew 10:7–8 NIrV

Jesus called His twelve disciples together to give them a special gift and an important mission. First, He gave them power to heal every sickness and drive out evil spirits that were hurting people. Then Jesus told them their special mission was to tell the good news about God's kingdom to the people of Israel. He said, "They are like sheep that have become lost. As you go, preach this message, 'The kingdom of heaven has come near.'" As part of their mission, Jesus told the disciples to heal people. Jesus had been kind to the disciples, and He wanted them to show the same kindness to others.

Jesus told the disciples some people would be happy to hear the good news they shared, but others would get angry. He told them to greet people as they traveled on their mission, but if people didn't welcome them, they should leave and move on.

TALK TO GOD
Ask the Holy Spirit to give you the right words to tell others about God's kingdom.

Jesus let the disciples know their mission wouldn't be easy. He said some of them would be punished by leaders for what they were doing. But Jesus promised, "When they arrest you, don't worry about what you will say or how you will say it. At that time you will be given the right words to say. . . . The Spirit of your Father will be speaking through you."

Just like the disciples, Jesus has given us a mission to tell people about God's kingdom. It may not be easy for us either, but we have the same Holy Spirit that the disciples had. When we accept Jesus's mission for our life, God will help us and speak through us to tell others how much He loves them.

EXPLORE MORE: What animals did Jesus tell the disciples to be like? Read Matthew 10:16 to find out.

DID YOU KNOW?

The book of Acts tells the stories of the disciples traveling around Israel and preaching the good news about Jesus. Many of the stories show how the disciples healed people with the power Jesus gave them.

I'm on a mission for Jesus.

God's Chosen Servant

"Here is my servant, the one I have chosen. He is the one I love, and I am very pleased with him." —Matthew 12:18 ERV

Many verses in the Old Testament point to Jesus. Some verses tell us where He would be born and the good names He would be called. God also gave the prophets messages to tell the people about the Messiah. God promised to send a Savior for the people and us.

In Matthew 12:18–21, Matthew shares verses about Jesus that were written by the prophet Isaiah more than seven hundred years earlier. In these verses, God tells us Jesus is the one God chose to save His people. God says, "Here is my servant, the one I have chosen. He is the one I love, and I am very pleased with Him." God said He would put His Spirit on Jesus, and many people would find their hope in Him.

TALK TO GOD
Ask God to show you how you can serve Him.

Did you know you are also one of God's chosen servants? If you believe in Jesus, then you are a child of God. You are chosen to serve Him. It might seem hard to know how to serve God while you are young, but the more you learn about God, the more you will understand how you can serve Him.

For example, you can serve God by serving others—like helping your brother or sister find their shoes or calling your grandma or grandpa just to say hi. You can serve God by being kind and playing with someone who is playing alone. If someone drops their markers, you can help pick them up. If you like to sing or play an instrument, you can serve God by praising Him.

It's impossible to list all the ways you can serve God, but you can ask Him to show you how. And as you serve God, you can thank Him for loving and choosing you.

EXPLORE MORE: What does Mark 10:45 tell us about Jesus?

I am one of God's chosen servants.

DID YOU KNOW?
Studies have shown that serving others can make us happier and more confident.

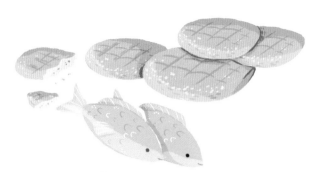

Jesus Feeds a Hungry Crowd

Jesus looked up and saw a large crowd coming toward him. He said to Philip, "Where can we buy bread for all these people to eat?" —John 6:5 ICB

Wherever Jesus went, large crowds followed Him. Many people had seen Jesus do miracles, like make sick people better. The crowds of people wanted to know more about Jesus and see what He would do next. One day Jesus walked up a hill and sat down with His disciples. He looked at the crowd and knew they were hungry. He asked His disciple, Philip, "Where can we buy bread for all these people to eat?" Jesus already knew what He was going to do, but He said this to see what Philip would say.

Philip knew it would be impossible to feed so many people. He said, "Someone would have to work almost a year to buy enough bread for each person here to have only a little piece."

Then Andrew said, "Here is a boy with five loaves of bread and two little fish. But that is not enough for so many people."

Jesus told the disciples to have the people sit down on the grass. Jesus took the bread and thanked God for it. Then He broke the bread and passed it around to all the people. He did the same thing with the fish. When everyone had finished eating, Jesus told His disciples to gather the leftover food.

The food they picked up was enough to fill twelve extra baskets.

Whenever Jesus performed a miracle, it was to show that He was God's Son—the One whom the prophets said would come. But He also did miracles to help people because He loved them. More than five thousand hungry people had enough to eat that day. The disciples didn't need to go into town to buy food, and they didn't need any money. In the same way, Jesus can give us what we need, and it's always enough.

TALK TO GOD
Thank God for giving you what you need each day.

DID YOU KNOW?
On November 13, 2008, Joaquim Goncalves of Brazil made the largest loaf of bread in history to celebrate Guinness World Records Day. The loaf weighed 3,463.46 pounds (1,571 kilograms).

EXPLORE MORE: Read John 6:14 to find out what the people said about Jesus when they saw this miracle.

Jesus gives me what I need.

Jesus Is the Living Bread

"I am the living bread that came down from heaven. Anyone who eats this bread will live forever; and this bread, which I will offer so the world may live, is my flesh." —John 6:51 NLT

People all over the world have been making and eating bread since the beginning of time. Did you know bread is often called the "staff of life" because for many people it's part of their daily meals? In Bible times, bread was usually made from wheat or barley because those were common grains in Israel. Today bread is also made from different flours like rice, potato, and almond.

We can read many stories about bread in the Bible. When the Israelites were in the wilderness, God sent manna, a type of bread, from heaven, so they could eat this special bread every day. When God told Elijah to hide out by the Kerith Ravine, God sent ravens to feed him with bread and meat. The prophet Elisha fed one hundred men with only twenty loaves of bread, and they even had some left over.

TALK TO GOD
Thank God for bread to eat and for eternal life from Jesus.

Bread was also used in the tabernacle and the temple. In Leviticus 24:5–9, God tells the people to bake twelve loaves of bread and set them in two stacks on the table of gold before the Lord. This bread needed to be baked every week, since the loaves provided food for the priests. The bread was a sign of the covenant agreement between God and His people.

John 6:33 says, "The true bread of God is the one who comes down from heaven and gives life to the world." The one who came down from heaven is Jesus. Just as bread gives us food for our daily lives, Jesus gives eternal life to those who believe and follow Him. Bread gives us food for our bodies, and Jesus gives us food for our souls.

EXPLORE MORE: Read what Jesus said in John 6:47–51.

Jesus is the bread that gives eternal life.

DID YOU KNOW?
Baking bread takes a lot of time, so many bread companies make enough to last for about a week. The color of the twist ties used to close the bags lets grocery store workers know which day of the week the bread was baked.

The Most Important Question

Then Jesus asked, "And who do you say I am? —Luke 9:20 ICB

People were amazed as Jesus taught the crowds and healed those who were sick, blind, deaf, or couldn't walk. Some wondered how Jesus could teach with so much wisdom. Others knew He had to have God's power to heal people from their diseases and disabilities. Others didn't believe He was the Son of God and wanted Him to go away.

One day as Jesus was alone praying, His disciples came to be with Him. Jesus asked them an important question: "Who do people say I am?"

"Some say you are John the Baptist," they replied. "Others say you are Elijah. And others say you are one of the prophets from long ago who has come back to life."

"And who do you say I am?" Jesus asked.

Peter was the first to answer Jesus's question. He said, "You are the Christ from God." Peter had seen Jesus do many miracles and heal lots of people. He had followed Jesus long enough to know that no one but God's Son could do the things that Jesus did.

TALK TO GOD
If you believe that Jesus is the Son of God, tell Him in your prayer, and ask Him to help you follow Him every day.

Did you know that many people today are like the people in the Bible? Some people think Jesus was a prophet. Some say He was a great teacher. Others say He was a good man. Jesus was all of those things, but He was and still is so much more.

Every person needs to answer the most important question, "Who is Jesus?" Peter gave the right answer. Jesus is the Christ, the Son of God. If you believe that, then you are a follower of Jesus.

DID YOU KNOW?
Some of the most common questions people ask are "How are you?" "What's your name?" and "Where are you from?"

EXPLORE MORE: What did the people in Jesus's hometown think about Him? Read Mark 6:1–3 to find out. The answer may surprise you!

Jesus is the Christ, the Son of God.

Tell What Jesus Has Done

At once the man was able to see, and he followed Jesus, thanking God. All the people who saw this praised God. —Luke 18:43 ICB

We don't know exactly how many blind people Jesus healed, but we know there were many! When Jesus made blind people able to see, the people who saw what happened were amazed, surprised, and confused. Many of Jesus's miracles were hard to explain and understand. Sometimes the only explanation was, "Jesus must be from God. That's why He can heal the blind!"

TALK TO GOD
Think of something Jesus has done for you, and say a prayer to thank Him.

Jesus's miracles showed His power over sickness, disease, disabilities, and even nature. And when people saw His miracles, they could not be quiet! News about Jesus's miracles spread quickly. When people heard these stories, they praised God. Many came to believe that Jesus truly was God's Son.

Even though Jesus isn't walking the earth today, He is still doing amazing things for us. He blesses families with children and grandchildren. He gives us wisdom to make good choices. He provides sunshine and rain for crops to grow, so we have good food to eat. And He promises a forever home in heaven to everyone who believes in Him.

Jesus does many wonderful things for us. The way to say "thank you" is to praise Him and tell others about Him. When you invite people to your home for dinner, you can say a prayer and ask God to bless your food. If you get a new brother or sister, you can tell others that God blessed your family with another child. You can also play music and sing songs that praise Jesus for His goodness and love. And on top of telling others about the wonderful things He has done for you, you can tell Jesus how much you appreciate all that He's done too.

EXPLORE MORE: After Jesus healed a man who was filled with demons, He told the man to do something. Read Luke 8:38–39 to see what it was.

I will tell others what Jesus does for me.

DID YOU KNOW?
Writing in a journal is a good way to remember what God does for you. Journaling helps your mind be more creative, and studies show that journaling at night helps you clear your mind and sleep better.

Two Sisters Welcome Jesus

"Only one thing is important. Mary has made the right choice, and it will never be taken away from her." —Luke 10:42 ERV

Jesus and His disciples traveled through a village where a woman named Martha invited Him to stay at her house. Martha had a sister named Mary who sat on the floor at Jesus's feet. Mary wanted to listen to everything Jesus had to say.

The Bible doesn't tell us exactly what Martha was doing, but it says that Martha was busy with work that needed to be done. Maybe she was cooking a big meal for Jesus and His disciples or preparing a comfortable room where Jesus could rest. What we do know is that Martha was upset because Mary wasn't helping her.

Martha said to Jesus, "Lord, don't you care that my sister has left me to do all the work by myself? Tell her to help me!"

Jesus's answer was not what Martha was expecting. "Martha, Martha, you are getting worried and upset about too many things. Only one thing is important. Mary has made the right choice and it will never be taken away from her."

TALK TO GOD
Think of something you want to tell Jesus, and talk about it in your prayer.

It's good to welcome people into your home and give them a meal and a place to rest. Serving others is a kind and generous thing to do. But Mary knew how special it was to have Jesus in her home. She wanted to spend every minute with Him and learn from Him.

Sometimes we get so busy that we forget to spend time with Jesus. But nothing is more important than learning from Him. No matter how busy you are today, take time to talk to Jesus and listen to His words in the Bible. It's always the best way to spend our time.

DID YOU KNOW?

Mary and Martha lived with their brother, Lazarus, in Bethany, which was a small town in Judea, near Jerusalem.

EXPLORE MORE: What did Jesus take time to do even when He was very busy? Read Luke 5:15–16 to find out.

I will take time to be with Jesus.

The Story of the Lost Sheep

"When he finds it, he will joyfully put it on his shoulders and go home." —Luke 15:5–6 NIrV

As people gathered around Jesus to listen to Him, the Jewish leaders and teachers of the law whispered among themselves. They criticized Jesus for spending time with tax collectors and people they thought of as sinners. Jesus knew what they were thinking, so He told a story.

"If a shepherd has one hundred sheep, and one sheep gets lost, won't he leave the ninety-nine sheep and go out to search for the one lost sheep? The shepherd will be so happy when he finds the sheep that he will carry it home on his shoulders. Then he will call his friends and neighbors and say, 'Be happy with me! I have found my lost sheep!'"

TALK TO GOD
Tell Jesus you are happy that He is your Shepherd.

Then Jesus explained the meaning of His story. He said, "It will be the same in heaven. There will be great joy when one sinner turns away from sin."

Just like the shepherd in Jesus's story searched for his lost sheep, Jesus searches for people who are spiritually lost. Being spiritually lost means someone doesn't believe that Jesus is God's Son and hasn't started following Him yet. When people decide to follow Jesus, they are no longer lost. This story shows us there is great joy in heaven if even one person becomes a Christian.

Every person is important to Jesus. He doesn't want anyone to be lost. Jesus is the Good Shepherd who gave His life for us, so we can be saved by believing in Him. If you believe in Jesus, then you are one of His sheep. And you can be happy every time one more lost sheep is found.

EXPLORE MORE: Isaiah 40:11 points to Jesus. How is this verse like today's story?

Jesus searches for people who are spiritually lost.

DID YOU KNOW?
When a sheep gets lost, it cannot find its way back home like some other animals can. That's why the shepherd needs to go out and find it.

Filled with Praise

He came into a small town, and ten men met him there. They did not come close to him, because they all had leprosy. But the men shouted, "Jesus! Master! Please help us!" —Luke 17:12–13 ERV

Another story of Jesus's healing power took place in a small village near Samaria and Galilee. This time it wasn't just one sick person who came to Jesus—it was ten men with leprosy. The men didn't dare come close to Jesus since people thought of them as being "unclean." But they shouted out to Him, "Jesus! Master! Please help us!"

When Jesus saw the men, He said, "Go and show your-selves to the priests." This is what people with leprosy had to do when they got better, so they could be around other people again. As the ten men went on their way, they were all healed. One of them, a Samaritan, looked at his skin and saw the amazing thing Jesus had done. He went back to Jesus and praised God with a loud voice. He bowed down before Jesus and thanked Him.

TALK TO GOD
Ask God to help you have a heart of thankfulness that praises Him.

Jesus said, "This man is not even one of our people. Is he the only one who came back to give praise to God?" Then Jesus told the man, "Stand up! You can go. You were healed because you believed."

All of the men did what Jesus told them to do and were healed, but only one was thankful enough to come back.

What can we do when Jesus does wonderful things for us and answers our prayers? We can be like the Samaritan in this story and let our hearts fill up with true praise. We can pray to Jesus or sing a song to tell Him how much we love Him and thank Him for being so kind.

EXPLORE MORE: Read Psalm 146:1–2. How long should we praise God?

DID YOU KNOW?
Samaritans were people who lived in Samaria. They were related to the Israelites, but the Jewish people didn't respect them like Jesus did.

I will be filled with praise.

The Resurrection and the Life

Jesus told her, "I am the resurrection and the life. Anyone who believes in me will live, even after dying." —John 11:25 NLT

Lazarus was the brother of Mary and Martha, and he was very sick. His sisters sent Jesus a message that Lazarus was not doing well. Jesus stayed where He was for two days and then traveled to Bethany to see them. When Jesus got there, someone told Him Lazarus had died and was buried four days earlier

Martha came to Jesus and said, "Lord, if only you had been here, my brother would not have died. But even now, I know that God will give you whatever you ask." Jesus told her, "Your brother will rise again." Martha answered, "Yes, he will rise when everyone else rises, at the last day." Then Jesus said something amazing: "I am the resurrection and the life. Anyone who believes in me will live, even after dying. Do you believe this, Martha?" Martha said she did because she believed that Jesus was the Messiah.

TALK TO GOD
Tell Jesus how powerful He is to conquer death and thank Him for being the Resurrection and the Life.

When Jesus saw Martha and Lazarus's friends crying, He was sad and cried too. He asked to see where Lazarus was buried. When He got to the tomb, He told the people to roll away the stone that covered the entrance. Jesus looked up to heaven and prayed out loud, so everyone could hear Him. Jesus shouted, "Lazarus, come out!" Then Lazarus walked out of the tomb, wrapped in graveclothes!

Jesus has power over death. What He did for Lazarus was incredible! What's even more wonderful is what He told Martha. Jesus promises that those who trust in Him will live with Him forever someday. He will raise our bodies from death just like He did for Lazarus, and we will never die again. Only Jesus can make that happen!

EXPLORE MORE: 1 Corinthians 15:51–52 says something amazing will happen to everyone who is a part of God's family. What is it?

Jesus has power over death.

DID YOU KNOW?
Bethany comes from the word *bethel*, which means House of God. Today the city of Bethany is called Al Eizariya, which means Place of Lazarus.

Jesus Loves the Little Children

Jesus saw what happened. He did not like his followers telling the children not to come. So he said to them, "Let the little children come to me. Don't stop them, because God's kingdom belongs to people who are like these little children." —Mark 10:14 ERV

Has anyone ever made you feel small because you're a kid? That's what happened to some kids in the Bible. Their parents brought them to Jesus so He could bless them. But the disciples told them to stop bringing their children to Jesus. Maybe they thought Jesus was too busy to spend time with kids.

Jesus saw what His disciples did, and He did not like it. He told His disciples, "Let the little children come to me. Don't stop them, because God's kingdom belongs to people who are like these little children." Then Jesus held the children in His arms and blessed them.

TALK TO GOD
Tell Jesus what you're feeling today. He wants to hear it!

Jesus told His followers that if they wanted to be a part of God's family, they needed to accept His kingdom the way kids accept things. That means trusting God the way kids trust their parents. Kids are happy to receive gifts and help from adults who love them. They don't feel like they have to earn everything on their own. That's how God's kingdom is. Jesus wants us to be happy to receive the gift He gives us by taking away our sins. He wants us to know it's something He did for us because He loves us. We can't earn this gift.

Just like the children in this story, you are important to Jesus. He loves you, and He wants you to come to Him. You can tell Him when you're feeling sad or when you're excited about something. And you can thank Him for the wonderful gifts He gives you. When grown-ups see you loving Jesus, it will teach them how to follow Him too.

EXPLORE MORE: What advice does 1 Timothy 4:12 have for kids?

DID YOU KNOW?
The song "Jesus Loves the Little Children" was written more than one hundred years ago. George Frederick Root composed the tune for another song, and later his friend, Clare Herbert Woolston, wrote the words. Woolston was inspired by today's story when he wrote the song.

I am important to Jesus.

The Loving Savior

Then Jesus talked to the 12 apostles alone. He said to them, "Listen! We are going to Jerusalem. Everything that God told the prophets to write about the Son of Man will happen!" —Luke 18:31 ICB

From the beginning, God's plan was to send Jesus to take away our sins. Even the prophets in the Old Testament told the people of Israel that it would happen. Because the sin of everyone in the world is so ugly and serious, God made a way for our sins to be forgiven through Jesus. Jesus knew the reason God sent Him to earth, and He was willing to die for us. Jesus knew what was going to happen to Him and when it would happen. He even told His disciples about it ahead of time. Jesus told them that He would be turned over to the Romans, and they would make fun of Him, spit on Him, and laugh at Him. They would even beat Him and kill Him. But Jesus also shared the wonderful part of His mission from God—He would rise from the dead three days later.

Even though the disciples heard everything Jesus said, they didn't understand what His mission was all about. They wouldn't be able to understand it until God gave them the ability to do so. God would help the disciples understand everything about Jesus's mission on earth after Jesus died.

Jesus wasn't surprised by the way He was treated or what happened to Him when He died. He knew all along that it was part of God's special plan to show His love to all of us. Jesus loves you enough that He was willing to die because it would bring you back to God. He is a kind and selfless Savior.

EXPLORE MORE: Read Genesis 3:15 to see that God already planned for Jesus to defeat Satan when Adam and Eve first sinned.

TALK TO GOD
Tell Jesus how grateful you are that He was willing to be made fun of and die to take away your sins.

DID YOU KNOW?
There are passages that talk about Jesus's death in Psalms, Isaiah, and Zechariah. Some of these passages were written more than six hundred years before Jesus was born.

Jesus came to die for the sins of the world.

Zacchaeus Wants to See Jesus

When Jesus came to where Zacchaeus was, he looked up and saw him in the tree. Jesus said, "Zacchaeus, hurry! Come down! I must stay at your house today." —Luke 19:5 ERV

Jesus was traveling through the city of Jericho. A tax collector named Zacchaeus lived there. You may remember that the Jewish people didn't like tax collectors because they often stole money from the taxes they took. Zacchaeus was a rich and important tax collector. He wanted to see Jesus, so he ran to a place where Jesus would pass by. But Zacchaeus was short and couldn't see over the crowds of people who also wanted to see Jesus, so Zacchaeus climbed a sycamore tree to get a good view.

When Jesus came to where Zacchaeus was, He saw Zacchaeus in the tree. Jesus called to him, "Zacchaeus, hurry! Come down! I must stay at your house today." Zacchaeus quickly came down the tree. He was happy for Jesus to stay at his house. Everyone who saw what was happening started to complain. "Look at the kind of man Jesus is staying with. Zacchaeus is a sinner!" they said.

Zacchaeus told Jesus, "I want to do good. I will give half of my money to the poor. If I have cheated anyone, I will pay them back four times more." Jesus answered, "Today is the day for this family to be saved from sin. Yes, even this tax collector is one of God's chosen people. The Son of Man came to find lost people and save them."

Even though other people judged Zacchaeus, Jesus knew that Zacchaeus wanted to know Him and was willing to change. Jesus didn't come for the people who think they are good enough to be saved, He came for everyone who wants to know and follow Him.

EXPLORE MORE: Do you remember the name of another tax collector who followed Jesus? Read Matthew 9:9 to see if you're right.

TALK TO GOD
Ask God to help you see people the way He sees them.

DID YOU KNOW?
Sycamore trees are the largest deciduous trees in the United States. Deciduous trees shed their leaves yearly. Sycamore trees can grow 75 to 100 feet (23 to 30 meters) tall.

Jesus sees those who want to know Him.

The Shepherd and the Gate

"I'm like a gate. Anyone who enters through me will be saved."
—John 10:9 NIrV

Back in Exodus, God told Moses His name was "I AM." Jesus also used this name to tell others that He was God's Son and part of the three persons of God—the Trinity. In the gospel of John, there are seven "I am" sayings from Jesus. One of them is: "I am the gate."

King David thought of God like a shepherd when he wrote Psalm 23. He even began with the words, "The Lord is my shepherd . . ." Jesus used the same example one day when He was talking with a group of Pharisees. He said that only the shepherd of a flock of sheep enters through the gate of a sheep pen. The sheep listen to the shepherd's voice. The shepherd calls every sheep by name and leads them out. Jesus said He was the Good Shepherd. Then Jesus said, "I am like a gate for the sheep. . . . Anyone who enters through me will be saved."

TALK TO GOD
Thank Jesus for making a way for us to get back to God.

When Jesus said this, He was explaining that He was the only way to God. Then He said, "I give my life for the sheep." This meant that He was going to die to save them. He also explained that there would be "one flock" and "one shepherd" in God's family, which means that everyone would be united in Jesus, no matter where they came from.

Jesus loves His people, and He knows them, just like a shepherd knows every sheep in his flock. Jesus came to take care of us, to lead us, and to protect us. Most of all, Jesus came so He could open the gate for all His followers to be made right with God. Jesus is the best shepherd we could ever have.

EXPLORE MORE: What did Jesus say in John 10:27–30?

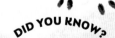

DID YOU KNOW?
The seven "I am" sayings of Jesus are I am the bread of life; I am the light of the world; I am the gate of the sheep; I am the resurrection and the life; I am the good shepherd; I am the way, the truth, and the life; and I am the true vine.

Jesus is the gate for His people.

Jesus Rides into Jerusalem

On the way to Jerusalem, many people spread their coats on the road for Jesus. Others cut branches from the trees and spread them on the road. —Matthew 21:8 ERV

As Jesus and His followers continued their trip to Jerusalem, they stopped at the Mount of Olives. Jesus sent two of His followers into town. He told them, "You will find a donkey with her colt. Untie them both and bring them to me. If anyone asks you why you are taking the donkeys, tell them 'The Master needs them.'"

His followers did what Jesus said. They brought the mother donkey and her colt back to Jesus. They covered the donkeys with their coats, and Jesus sat on them. As they traveled to Jerusalem, crowds of people spread their coats on the road to honor Him as a King. They shouted, "Praise to the Son of David! Welcome! God bless the one who comes in the name of the Lord! Praise to God in heaven!" Some of the Pharisees saw what was happening, and they told Jesus, "Teacher, tell your followers not to say these things." But Jesus answered, "I tell you, if my followers didn't say them, these stones would shout them." No one could hold back the royal praise that Jesus deserved.

Back in the Old Testament, Jesus's entrance into Jerusalem was described exactly like this by the prophet Zechariah. He told the Israelites their king would come humble and riding on a donkey. Jesus didn't come as a warrior on a horse, trying to take over the world by fighting wars. He came as a servant out of love to make us right with God and show us how He wants us to live. He is the perfect King and worthy of all of our praise.

TALK TO GOD
Thank Jesus for coming as a humble King who showed love to the world.

EXPLORE MORE: Go back and read the prophecy of Jesus entering Jerusalem in Zechariah 9:9.

DID YOU KNOW?
In some translations of the Bible, the word *Hosanna* is used in today's story. *Hosanna* is a Hebrew word that the Israelites shouted to praise Jesus as He entered Jerusalem. It means "joy," "adoration," or "praise" and was also used in praying to God for help.

Jesus, the humble King, deserves all our praise.

A Very Special Supper

When the time came, Jesus and the apostles were sitting at the table. He said to them, "I wanted very much to eat this Passover meal with you before I die." —Luke 22:14–15 ICB

After Jesus and His disciples arrived in Jerusalem, it was time to celebrate the Day of Unleavened Bread. On this day Passover lambs were sacrificed, and the people remembered what God did for their ancestors in Egypt at the first Passover. Jesus told Peter and John, "Go and prepare the Passover meal for us." They asked, "Where do you want us to prepare it?" Jesus said they would see a man carrying a jar of water. When they followed him to a house, the owner would show them a room. Peter and John left, and everything happened the way Jesus said it would.

TALK TO GOD
Thank Jesus for giving His life for yours.

At dinner, Jesus sat with His twelve disciples. He said, "I wanted very much to eat this Passover meal with you before I die." Then Jesus took some bread and thanked God for it. He broke it, gave it to His disciples, and said, "This bread is my body that I am giving for you. Do this to remember me." After dinner, Jesus took a cup and said that God was making a new agreement with His people. "This new agreement begins with my blood which is poured out for you."

The special meal Jesus ate with His disciples is called the Last Supper. It was the last time He ate with them before He died. The bread and cup were symbols that showed Jesus was going to give His life for all who believed in Him. This Passover meal was also special because Jesus is the Lamb of God. His blood saves us from punishment, like the lamb's blood saved the Israelites in Egypt. Jesus is a kind and loving Savior.

EXPLORE MORE: Read Joshua 5:10 to see what Joshua and the Israelites did after crossing the Jordan River.

DID YOU KNOW?
Today people remember the Last Supper when they take communion or the Lord's Supper at church. They break bread or crackers and drink juice or wine to remember what Jesus told His followers on that special night.

Jesus is the Lamb of God.

An Unexpected Foot Bath

So while they were eating, Jesus stood up and took off his robe. He got a towel and wrapped it around his waist. —John 13:4 ERV

After Jesus and His followers entered Jerusalem, Jesus knew the time had come for Him to leave the world and go back to the Father. He ate a special dinner with His followers, and while they were eating, He stood up and poured water into a bowl. Then He began to wash their feet. When Jesus got to Peter, Peter said, "Lord, you should not wash my feet." Jesus answered, "If I don't wash your feet, you are not one of my people."

When Jesus finished washing His disciples' feet, He went back to the table and asked them, "Do you understand what I did for you? You call me 'Teacher.' And you call me 'Lord.' And this is right, because that is what I am. But I washed your feet. So you also should wash each other's feet. You should serve each other just as I served you."

The disciples were probably surprised by what Jesus did. Washing someone's feet was the job of the least important servant in the house. Jesus told His disciples to serve others and to not think of themselves as better than others. Jesus was different from what most people expected the Messiah to be like. Instead of coming into the world as a powerful king in a fancy palace, He was a humble servant who cared about people that others looked down on.

When we believe in Jesus, He washes our sins away, just like how He washed the disciples' feet. When our hearts are changed by Jesus's love, we take His love and share it with others by serving them with kindness.

EXPLORE MORE: Read John 13:1 to find out what Jesus did until the very end of His life on earth.

TALK TO GOD
Ask God to show you how to be a servant like Jesus.

DID YOU KNOW?
People had to wash their feet a lot in Bible times because they wore sandals and walked on dusty roads. A servant or the wife of the host usually washed guests' feet when they came over for dinner.

Jesus shows me how to be a servant.

The Only Way

Thomas said to Jesus, "Lord, we don't know where you are going. So how can we know the way?" Jesus answered, "I am the way. And I am the truth and the life. The only way to the Father is through me." —John 14:5–6 ICB

As Jesus continued His special dinner with His disciples, He didn't want them to be confused or scared about the things that were going to happen. He wanted them to know He still cared about them. Jesus said, "Don't let your hearts be troubled. Trust in God. And trust in me." Then He told His disciples that He was going to His Father's house to get a place ready for them. He said He would come back and take them to be with Him. Jesus told them, "You know the way to the place where I am going." But Thomas said, "Lord, we don't know where you are going. So how can we know the way?" Jesus replied, "I am the way. And I am the truth and the life. The only way to the Father is through me."

Jesus explained to His disciples His amazing and true plan, even if they didn't understand it right away. He let them know He was going back to heaven to get His kingdom ready. He promised to come back and bring all of His followers to His new kingdom.

TALK TO GOD
Praise Jesus for being the way to God.

Jesus's death on the cross made a way for all sinners to get back to God if they believe in Jesus. He is the only way to be made right with God. When we accept Jesus's free gift of saving us from our sins, it's like He creates a bridge from us to God. This bridge leads us back to God, who created us and loves us.

EXPLORE MORE: What did Peter say to some Jewish leaders after he healed a crippled man? Read Acts 4:12 to find out.

DID YOU KNOW?
The Apostle Islands National Lakeshore on Lake Superior in Wisconsin is named after the twelve disciples, or apostles, and has twenty-one islands. There's only one way to get to the islands and that is by boat.

Jesus is the only way to God.

Growing Grapes

"I am the vine. You are the branches. If you remain joined to me, and I to you, you will bear a lot of fruit. You can't do anything without me." —John 15:5 NIrV

Did you know grapevines were everywhere in Israel? Lots of grapes grew in vineyards, and vines were a symbol of God's people in the Old Testament. There was even a large golden vine on the front of the temple.

One day Jesus taught a parable about a vineyard. Jesus used the symbol of a vine to teach His disciples. He said, "I am the vine. You are the branches. If you remain joined to me, and I to you, you will bear a lot of fruit. You can't do anything without me. . . . When you bear a lot of fruit, it brings glory to my Father."

Did Jesus mean that His followers would have grapes hanging off their arms? That would definitely be something everyone would remember! But that's not what Jesus meant. As we've seen in other stories, Jesus liked to use symbols to teach people. The symbol of fruit was the work of Jesus in the disciples' hearts showing on the outside—things like being patient, kind, gentle and loving, and having joy, peace, and self-control. All of Jesus's followers grow this fruit when they stay close to Him.

TALK TO GOD
Tell Jesus you want to stay close to Him and ask Him to grow His fruit in your life.

When we don't stay close to Jesus, we can't grow His fruit, just like a branch that falls off a tree can't grow leaves. That's what Jesus meant when He said we can't do anything without Him. God doesn't expect us to do all the work on our own. He wants to help us and has given us everything we need through the Holy Spirit. When we stay close to Him and that fruit shows up in our lives, it gives all the glory back to God. What delicious fruit!

EXPLORE MORE: Read John 15:1. If Jesus is the vine, who is the gardener?

DID YOU KNOW?
Israel is only the size of New Jersey, but there are hundreds of vineyards in Israel today. There are 70 vineyards that produce 50 tons (45,359 kilograms or 100,000 pounds) of grapes in a year.

Jesus is the vine.

The Savior's Prayer

After Jesus said these things he looked toward heaven. Jesus prayed, "Father, the time has come. Give glory to your Son so that the Son can give glory to you." —John 17:1 ICB

Jesus went to a garden to pray. He told Peter, James, and John that His heart was breaking with sadness. He knew He was about to die on the cross for the sins of the world. But even with everything Jesus was going through, do you know what He prayed for? He prayed for His disciples, and He prayed for *you*. That's right—Jesus was thinking of you on that quiet night in the garden thousands of years ago.

First Jesus prayed for the twelve disciples who had followed Him. He said, "I want them to have all of my joy. I have given them your teaching." Then He asked God to keep them safe from the Evil One and to make them ready to serve and teach God's truth.

Then Jesus prayed for people who would believe in Him. If you know Jesus, that's you! He asked God, "Father, I pray that all people who believe in me can be one . . . I pray that these people can also be one in us, so that the world will believe that you sent me." Jesus also said, "I want them to see my glory . . . I showed them what you are like . . . they will have the same love that you have for me, and I will live in them."

How amazing that Jesus thought of us the night before He died! And it's wonderful to see Jesus's prayers have been answered. We see Jesus's glory in the world He made, in His Spirit living inside of us, and in the way He hears our prayers and changes our hearts. The best way we can keep shining Jesus's glory is by loving each other with God's love.

TALK TO GOD
Tell Jesus how thankful you are that He prayed for you, and ask Him to help you honor His name.

EXPLORE MORE: What does Hebrews 7:25 tell us about Jesus?

Jesus prayed for me.

DID YOU KNOW?
The garden where Jesus prayed was called Gethsemane, which means "oil press" in Hebrew. It was probably a grove of olive trees with an oil press in it for making olive oil.

Another Prayer in the Garden

Jesus and his followers went to a place called Gethsemane. He said to his followers, "Sit here while I pray." —Mark 14:32 ICB

Jesus brought His disciples to a garden by the Mount of Olives in Jerusalem. The garden was filled with olive trees. The place was called Gethsemane. Jesus told the disciples to sit and wait while He went by himself to pray. He walked a little farther with Peter, James, and John, then told them to watch and pray. When Jesus was alone, He dropped to the ground. His heart was sad as He talked to God. He prayed, "Abba, Father! You can do all things. Let me not have this cup of suffering. But do what you want, not what I want."

Jesus got up and walked back to the disciples and found them sleeping. He woke them up and told them again to watch and pray. Jesus went back to pray by himself. When He returned to the disciples, they were sleeping. This happened a third time too. Then a group of men came to the garden. They were the Roman soldiers who had come to arrest Jesus and take Him away. Judas, who was one of Jesus's disciples, kissed Jesus on the cheek. This was a sign to the soldiers that Jesus was the man they were looking for.

TALK TO GOD
Thank Jesus for obeying God's will, so you can be saved from your sins.

The soldiers were sent by the Jewish chief priests and teachers of the law. They were armed with swords and clubs, but they didn't have to use them. Jesus didn't put up a fight or perform a miracle to escape. He went along willingly because He knew this was God's plan.

Jesus knew the days ahead would be filled with pain and suffering, but He wanted to do God's will and make a way for us to be saved.

EXPLORE MORE: What happened to Jesus as He was praying? Read Luke 22:43–44 to find out.

DID YOU KNOW?
According to a 2012 study by the Italian National Research Council, three of the olive trees in Gethsemane are among the oldest trees in the world.

Jesus did what God wanted Him to do.

Jesus and Pilate

Jesus answered, "You are right to say that I am a king. I was born for this: to tell people about the truth. That is why I came into the world. And everyone who belongs to the truth listens to me." —John 18:37 ERV

The Roman guards took Jesus to the governor's palace. His name was Pilate. Some Jewish leaders went with Jesus but stayed outside. Pilate went out and asked the leaders, "What has this man done wrong?"

"He's a bad man," they said. "That's why we brought Him to you."

Pilate took Jesus into the palace and asked Him some questions. "Are you the king of the Jews?" he asked. "Your people and their leaders brought you to me. What have you done wrong?"

"My kingdom does not belong to this world," Jesus said. "If it did, my servants would fight so that I would not be handed over to the Jewish leaders. My kingdom is not an earthly one."

"So you are a king," Pilate said.

"You are right to say that I am a king," Jesus replied. "I was born for this: to tell people about the truth. That is why I came into the world. And everyone who belongs to the truth listens to me."

TALK TO GOD
Ask Jesus to help you stand up for Him no matter what.

Pilate could not find a reason to punish Jesus. He asked the people if they wanted him to let Jesus go free or to let a criminal named Barabbas go free. The Jews chose Barabbas.

Pilate knew Jesus hadn't done anything wrong, but he was afraid of the crowd. Instead of standing up for Jesus, Pilate handed Jesus over to be crucified.

We should be willing to stand up for Jesus no matter what others say or do. It might be hard, and others might even laugh at us. But standing up for Jesus is always the right thing to do because Jesus always stands up for us.

EXPLORE MORE: Read Matthew 27:19 to find out what Pilate's wife said to him.

I will stand up for Jesus.

DID YOU KNOW?

"Stand Up, Stand Up for Jesus" is a hymn that was written in 1858 by a Presbyterian minister named George Duffield. He was inspired to write the song when a preacher named Dudley Tyng said in a sermon, "Let us stand up for Jesus."

Jesus Is Crucified

They put a sign above Jesus' head with the charge against him written on it. The sign read: "THIS IS JESUS THE KING OF THE JEWS."
—Matthew 27:37 ICB

After Pilate handed Jesus over to the Roman soldiers, they put a robe on Him and made a crown of thorns for His head. They put a staff in His hand and got down on their knees. "Hail, king of the Jews," they said as they made fun of Him. They spit on Jesus and hit Him with the staff. Then they led Him away to be crucified.

The soldiers took Jesus to a place outside the city gates of Jerusalem called Golgotha. They met a man named Simon from Cyrene and made him carry Jesus's cross. Then the soldiers nailed Jesus's hands and feet to the cross and stood it up on a hill. Two criminals were crucified next to Jesus, one on each side.

As people walked by, they yelled mean things at Jesus. "Come down from the cross if you're really the Son of God!" they said. "He saved others, but He can't save himself! If He's the King of Israel, let Him come down from the cross and we will believe in Him!"

TALK TO GOD
Thank God for sending Jesus to die for our sins and take our place.

Jesus had the power to come down from the cross at any time. He could have performed a thousand miracles to prove that He was the Son of God. But that was not God's plan. Jesus had to die on the cross because He is the Lamb of God who sacrificed His life for ours. God showed His greatest love for us by sending Jesus to die for our sins. We deserve to be punished for our sins, but we are set free because Jesus took our place.

EXPLORE MORE: Read Luke 23:39–43 to find out what the criminals said as they hung on a cross next to Jesus.

DID YOU KNOW?
Golgotha means "The Place of the Skull." Jerusalem was considered a holy city, so Golgotha was a place where they crucified criminals. It's also where they brought the remains of animals that were sacrificed.

Jesus was crucified for me.

Jesus Dies

**When Jesus died, the curtain in the Temple was torn into two pieces. The tear started at the top and tore all the way to the bottom. Also, the earth shook and rocks were broken.
—Matthew 27:51 ERV**

As Jesus hung on the cross, the sky became dark for three hours. Jesus said He was thirsty, so the soldiers soaked a sponge in vinegar and lifted it to His lips. Then He cried out, "My God, my God, why have you forsaken me?" When Jesus cried out these words, He took our sins upon himself and showed how sin separates us from God.

Jesus's last words on the cross were, "It is finished." Then Jesus died. At that moment the curtain in the temple was torn in two from top to bottom. This showed that our sin no longer separates us from God. Because of Jesus's death on the cross, we can be in God's presence. Jesus's death on the cross made a way for people to be cleansed from their sins.

When Jesus died, the earth shook, and rocks split apart. Some of the tombs opened up, and people who had died came out. The guards who saw what happened were terrified. They said, "He really was the Son of God!"

A rich man named Joseph was a follower of Jesus. He was from the town of Arimathea. He asked Pilate for Jesus's body, and Pilate agreed. Joseph wrapped Jesus's body in new linen cloths and placed Him in a tomb that he had dug in a wall of rock. He put a large stone over the opening of the tomb.

TALK TO GOD
Thank God that everything that happened to Jesus was part of His plan.

The Jewish leaders remembered how Jesus said He would rise from the dead on the third day, so they told Pilate to make sure the tomb was sealed and guarded. But the people would soon find out that nothing can stop God's plan.

EXPLORE MORE: Who were some other followers watching Jesus that day? Read Matthew 27:55–56 to find out.

Jesus really is the Son of God.

DID YOU KNOW?
Joseph of Arimathea was a Jewish leader. He is only mentioned in this story, but Matthew, Mark, Luke, and John all include him in their gospels.

He Isn't Here!

"He isn't here! He is risen from the dead, just as he said would happen. Come, see where his body was lying." —Matthew 28:6 NLT

Early on Sunday morning, Mary Magdalene and Mary the mother of James went to the tomb where Jesus was buried. They wanted to put spices on Jesus's body but wondered how they would move the heavy stone. Suddenly, the earth shook, and an angel came down from heaven and rolled the stone away from the tomb. The angel's face and clothing were as bright as lightning. The guards standing watch at the tomb were so frightened they fell to the ground.

The angel said to the women, "Don't be afraid. I know you are looking for Jesus, who was crucified. He is not here. He has risen just like He said. Come and see where His body was lying. Then go tell His disciples, 'Jesus has risen from the dead.'"

The women were frightened but filled with joy! They ran to tell the disciples what the angel had said, and on their way, they met Jesus. He said to them, "Don't be afraid. Tell my brothers to go to Galilee, and I will see them there."

When the guards realized what had happened, they went to Jerusalem and told the Jewish leaders. The leaders had a meeting and decided to pay the guards a lot of money to lie. They told the soldiers, "Tell everyone Jesus's disciples came during the night and stole His body while you were sleeping." The guards agreed and took the money.

TALK TO GOD
Ask God to help you believe the truth that is in the Bible.

The people who didn't believe that Jesus was God's Son had to make up lies because they didn't want to accept the truth. Jesus's followers believed that Jesus was the Son of God, and now they would believe that He had come back to life.

EXPLORE MORE: What did the disciples think when the women told them about the empty tomb? Read Luke 24:9–12 to find out.

DID YOU KNOW?
During the time of Jesus, the stones that were used to seal a tomb were about 4 to 6 feet (1.2 to 1.8 meters) tall and weighed 1.5 to 2 tons (1,361 to 1,814 kilograms). It was very hard to roll the stone away because it sat in a groove in the ground.

Jesus came back to life, just like He said He would.

No More Doubts

Then Jesus told him, "You believe because you have seen me. Blessed are those who believe without seeing me." —John 20:29 NLT

Even though Jesus had told His disciples He would rise from the dead on the third day, they were still confused. Not all of them believed that Jesus was alive. In the evening they were meeting together with the doors locked because they were afraid of the Jewish leaders. Suddenly, Jesus stood before them. "Peace be with you!" He said. Jesus showed them the wounds in His hands and feet. The disciples were filled with joy when they saw Him. They no longer doubted that Jesus was alive.

Thomas, one of Jesus's twelve disciples, was not with them. When the disciples told them they saw Jesus, He didn't believe them. Thomas said, "I won't believe it unless I see the nail wounds in His hands, put my fingers into them, and place my hand into the wound in His side."

TALK TO GOD
Thank God that we never have to doubt the words in the Bible because we know they are true.

Eight days later the disciples were meeting again with the doors locked, and Thomas was with them. Suddenly, Jesus stood before them, just like before. "Peace be with you," He said. Then He said to Thomas, "Put your finger here, and look at my hands. Put your hand into the wound in my side. Don't doubt anymore. Just believe!"

Thomas didn't need any more proof. He said out loud, "My Lord and my God!" He saw with his own eyes that Jesus was alive. Jesus said, "You believe because you have seen me. Blessed are those who believe without seeing me."

We cannot see Jesus right now, but someday we will see Him face to face. The Bible tells us it's true, so we don't have to doubt. We can just believe!

EXPLORE MORE: What does John tell us in John 20:31?

I believe I will see Jesus.

DID YOU KNOW?
Thomas also went by the name Didymus, which is a Greek name that means "the twin," but the Bible doesn't tell us whether or not Thomas was a twin.

Breakfast on the Beach

Jesus said to them, "Come and have breakfast." None of the disciples dared to ask him, "Who are you?" They knew it was the Lord. —John 21:12 NIrV

One night after Jesus's resurrection, Peter and Thomas decided to go fishing. Some of the other disciples went with them. They fished all night and didn't catch anything. Early in the morning, a man was standing on shore. He called out, "Friends, don't you have any fish?"

"No," they answered. The disciples didn't realize the man was Jesus.

"Throw your net on the right side of the boat," He said. "There you will find some fish."

When they did, their net was bursting with fish. "It's the Lord!" John said. Peter jumped in the water while the other disciples followed in the boat, towing the net full of fish.

When they reached the shore, they saw fish cooking over a fire of burning coals and some bread. Jesus told them to bring some of the fish they had caught, so Peter went to the boat and dragged the net to shore. Jesus said, "Come and have breakfast." He took the fish and bread and gave it to the disciples to eat.

Even though Jesus had finished what God sent Him to do, He wanted to encourage His followers and serve them. He even called them His friends. Soon, He would no longer be with them in person, but He would always be with them in spirit. More than anything else, Jesus loved His followers and wanted them to tell the world about Him—the Son of God they had come to know.

TALK TO GOD
Ask God to help you learn more about Him every day.

Jesus is your friend too. The more time you spend with Him, the more you will get to know Him. And you can even talk to Him when you eat your breakfast!

EXPLORE MORE: Read John 21:11 to find out how many fish were in the disciples' net.

DID YOU KNOW?
Israeli breakfasts are considered one of the healthiest breakfasts in the world. In Israel people eat eggs, fruits, vegetables, salads, breads, fish, and cheese for breakfast.

I want to know Jesus more.

So Much More

Jesus also did many other things. What if every one of them were written down? I suppose that even the whole world would not have room for the books that would be written. —John 21:25 NIrV

Matthew, Mark, Luke, and John are four books in the Bible called the Gospels. They talk about the birth and life of Jesus when He was on the earth. They tell us about Jesus's travels through different towns and villages and how He taught and healed many people. These books include about thirty-seven miracles that Jesus performed and forty-three parables that He shared. He also taught many sermons and prayed many prayers. All of this took place in about three and a half years.

John, who was one of Jesus's disciples, wrote the gospel of John in the Bible. In the last verse of the last chapter, he writes something that's pretty amazing. John 21:25 says, "Jesus also did many other things. What if every one of them were written down? I suppose that even the whole world would not have room for the books that would be written."

John is saying that it's impossible to keep a record of everything Jesus did because He did so many things. The Holy Spirit guided the writers to write down the things God wanted us to know. When we read about Jesus's miracles and parables and the things He taught His followers, we can be amazed at everything He did. And He did so much more!

TALK TO GOD
Thank God for the Gospels, so we can learn about Jesus's life on earth.

John was there when Jesus showed love and compassion for others. He saw Jesus walk on water and calm the storms. He watched Jesus use His power to heal the sick and raise people from the dead. John listened to Jesus's parables and followed Him everywhere. John knew how great Jesus is, and he wanted everyone else to know it too, including you!

EXPLORE MORE: Why can we believe what John said about Jesus? You can find the answer in John 21:24.

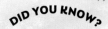

Jesus did too many things to write in books.

Go and Make Disciples

So you must go and make disciples of all nations. Baptize them in the name of the Father and of the Son and of the Holy Spirit.
—Matthew 28:19 NIrV

The disciples went to Galilee to meet Jesus at a mountain where He gave them an important message. First, He said, "All authority in heaven and earth has been given to me." That means Jesus has power and control over everything, and He can use His power to help His followers do great things.

Then Jesus said, "Go and make disciples of all nations." The gospel message was first given to the Jews, but even during Jesus's time on earth, people from other nations were given the chance to believe in Him. Jesus wanted His disciples to bring the message of salvation to *all* people *everywhere*.

TALK TO GOD
Ask God to help you spread His message of love and salvation wherever you go.

Then Jesus said, "Baptize them in the name of the Father and of the Son and of the Holy Spirit." Baptism is a sign that people choose to follow Jesus and have asked Him to forgive their sins. Their old life is in the past, and they have a new life as they follow Jesus.

The next thing Jesus said was, "Teach them to obey everything I have commanded you." Jesus taught His disciples how to love God and others. Now He wanted them to teach others everything that He taught them.

Jesus ended His message with an important promise. "And you can be sure that I am always with you, to the very end." Jesus was going back to heaven, but He would not leave them alone. He promised to send the Holy Spirit to give them the courage to teach and the right words to say.

Jesus's message is also for us. Anyone who believes in Jesus is His disciple, and He wants us to make more disciples wherever we go.

EXPLORE MORE: Some of Jesus's last words are also found in Acts 1:8. Read it to see what Jesus said.

DID YOU KNOW?
The verses in Matthew 28:18–20 are called "The Great Commission." This was the last command Jesus gave His disciples before He went to heaven. A commission is a special duty given to a group of people.

Jesus wants me to make disciples.

Jesus Goes to Heaven

After Jesus said this, he was lifted up into the sky. While they were watching, he went into a cloud, and they could not see him. —Acts 1:9 ERV

After Jesus came back to life, He lived on earth for forty days. He appeared to His disciples many times to prove that He had risen from the dead. When it was time for Jesus to leave for heaven, He gave His followers special directions. It was time for them to do the work Jesus had started.

After He told His disciples what to do, Jesus rose into the sky. A cloud covered Jesus, and the disciples could no longer see Him. As they kept looking into the sky, two men wearing white clothes came and spoke to them. "Men from Galilee," they said, "why are you standing here looking into the sky? You saw Jesus carried away from you into heaven. He will come back in the same way you saw him go." From that day on—even until today—Jesus's followers have important directions to follow. We are called to share God's love with others everywhere. We can follow Jesus's example of being kind and helping our friends, neighbors, and other people we meet. We can invite people to church, give them a Bible, or tell them the story of Jesus. We can spread the news that Jesus is our Savior—the Messiah that God promised to send. And everyone who believes in Jesus will have a forever life with Him.

TALK TO GOD
Thank Jesus that He is coming back someday. Ask Him to help you follow Him now.

Jesus came to earth so He could sacrifice His life for our sins. He went back to heaven, but that is not the end of the story. Jesus will come again someday to be the King over all the earth.

EXPLORE MORE: What did the disciples do after Jesus went to heaven? Read Luke 24:50–53 to find the answer.

Jesus is coming back someday.

DID YOU KNOW?
The day Jesus went to heaven is called Ascension Day. It is still celebrated around the world, forty days after the celebration of Jesus's resurrection. In many countries it is a public holiday.

The Holy Spirit Comes

They were all filled with the Holy Spirit, and they began to speak different languages. The Holy Spirit was giving them the power to do this. —Acts 2:4 ERV

One day as Jesus's followers were meeting together several weeks after Jesus ascended to heaven, a noise filled the house. It sounded like a strong wind blowing. Then small flames of fire appeared and stood above everyone there. The believers were filled with the Holy Spirit and began speaking in languages they did not know. The Holy Spirit gave them the power to do this amazing thing.

Jewish people from every country were staying in Jerusalem at that time. Many of them came to the house where Jesus's followers were because they had heard the sound of wind and wanted to see what was happening. They were surprised when they heard the disciples speaking in different languages. Everyone heard someone speaking their own language, and they didn't know how that was possible. "These men are from Galilee," they said. "How can they be speaking our languages? We can all understand the great things they are saying about God!"

TALK TO GOD
Thank God for the gift of the Holy Spirit, who is our helper, teacher, and comforter.

Once Jesus's followers had received the Holy Spirit, they had the power to spread the gospel throughout the whole world. The Holy Spirit would also fill them with wisdom and truth. The Holy Spirit would give them patience, peace, and comfort as they faced many challenges. Jesus had promised the Holy Spirit would come, and His promises are true.

Everyone who believes in Jesus as their Savior receives the gift of the Holy Spirit. The Holy Spirit helps us know what God wants us to do and gives us the wisdom and strength to do it. He comforts us when we are sad and guides us as we live. Jesus doesn't want us to be alone, so He sent the Holy Spirit to be with us.

DID YOU KNOW?
The day the Holy Spirit came is known as Pentecost. It comes from the Greek word *pentekoste* which means "fiftieth." Pentecost is celebrated fifty days after Easter.

EXPLORE MORE: Look up Acts 2:9–11 to read a list of all the different places the people were from who heard the disciples speaking their own languages.

Jesus gives the Holy Spirit to everyone who believes in Him.

One True Gospel

There is no other message that is the Good News, but some people are confusing you. They want to change the Good News about Christ. —Galatians 1:7 ERV

The word *gospel* means "good news." As you read through the Bible, you can see why it's such good news that Jesus came to save us from our sins. And that's why Paul and the first Christians wanted to spread the gospel message around the world.

Today's Scripture is from a letter to a church in a place called Galatia. The Christians in Galatia tried to follow God, but they believed some confusing messages from false teachers. Paul heard about what was happening and sent a letter to remind them of the truth. The false teachers told the Galatians they had to do certain things to be made right with God. They said they needed to do more than believe in Christ. The false teachers were adding to the gospel of Jesus's death and resurrection. Paul explained that these teachers were trying to change the gospel by telling people they had to do more than believe in Jesus to be saved.

TALK TO GOD
Ask God to help you know His truth by studying His Word.

There are still religions in the world today that change the gospel message. How can we tell which messages are true? By following what the Bible says! The Bible shows us the way to God. It tells us believing in Jesus is the only way to be saved from our sins. Anyone or any religion that says something different isn't the true gospel. There is only one gospel message: Jesus is the Son of God, who came to earth, died on the cross, and was raised again, so we can have eternal life. That's the best news of all!

EXPLORE MORE: Read the gospel message Paul shared in 1 Corinthians 15:1–4.

There is only one true gospel.

DID YOU KNOW?
Galatia was an area in the north-central part of modern-day Turkey. It was settled by the Celtic Gauls, which is where the name Galatia comes from.

Free in Jesus

Christ has set us free to enjoy our freedom. So remain strong in the faith. —Galatians 5:1 NIrV

When you're a kid, there are lots of rules to follow. Your parents have rules about what time you have to go to bed and when you can have screen time. Your teachers have rules at school and tell you when you can talk and when you have to listen. If you play on a sports team, there are rules to play the game. Even though rules keep you safe and help you learn, sometimes they can be hard to follow.

Some people think being a Christian means following a long list of rules. They may not understand what the Bible says. These people think they have to do or not do certain things for God to accept them. Thinking this way goes all the way back to the first Christians Paul taught about Jesus. Paul said to the Galatians, "Some of you are trying to be made right with God by obeying the law. . . . But we long to be made completely holy because of our faith in Christ." Paul explained that Jesus's sacrifice on the cross set us free from having to follow lots of rules like the Israelites in the Old Testament. No one can keep God's law perfectly. Jesus came so we didn't have to keep the law perfectly.

Believing in Jesus's sacrifice for us takes away our sin; it doesn't mean we have to follow a bunch of rules to be good enough. Jesus gave us His goodness instead. When we trust in Him, we are made right with God, and we can enjoy our lives, knowing we are free and right with God.

EXPLORE MORE: What did Paul tell the Galatians to do with their freedom in Galatians 5:13–14?

> **TALK TO GOD**
> Thank Jesus that He has given you freedom from sin.

> **DID YOU KNOW?**
> One of the most common rules parents give in the United States is "always say please and thank you." After that it's "always be kind" and "you have to finish your homework before you can play."

Jesus sets me free.

Saved by Grace

God's grace has saved you because of your faith in Christ. Your salvation doesn't come from anything you do. It is God's gift.
—Ephesians 2:8 NIrV

Nothing could stop Paul from telling others about Jesus. Even when he was in prison, he kept preaching about Jesus to the guards and other prisoners. When he was in prison, Paul also wrote letters to Christians in different cities. He wanted the believers to become more like Jesus by showing kindness and love to each other.

In Paul's letter to the Ephesians, he reminded them that because of God's great love, they were saved from sin by His grace. Do you know what grace means? It's getting something wonderful that you don't deserve. It's like getting the best present you've ever received just because someone loves you. Paul wanted Christians to understand that believing in Jesus is what saves them. Salvation from sin is a gift from God, and not something anyone can earn by doing good things. That message is not just for the Ephesians; it's for everyone.

Some people think they have to do good things to go to heaven, but that's not what the Bible tells us. No one is good enough to earn their salvation, which is why God sent Jesus to die for us. Salvation is a gift we don't deserve. But because of God's grace, He gives salvation from sin to everyone who believes in Jesus.

Aren't you glad you don't have to work hard to earn your way to heaven? You can just accept God's gift and enjoy living for Jesus. You can follow Jesus's example of being kind and loving to everyone—and that includes your friends, family, neighbors, and new people you meet. Being kind to others shows the love of Jesus in your heart.

EXPLORE MORE: Read Ephesians 2:7 to learn more about God's grace.

TALK TO GOD
Thank God that we can be saved by believing in Jesus.

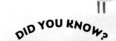

DID YOU KNOW?
Ephesians, Philippians, Colossians, and Philemon are four letters Paul wrote while he was in prison that became books of the Bible. For this reason, they are sometimes called the "Prison Epistles," or prison letters.

Jesus saves me by God's grace.

God's Message

And now in these last days God has spoken to us through his Son. God has chosen his Son to own all things. And he made the world through the Son. —Hebrews 1:2 ICB

In the Old Testament we read about prophets God spoke through to carry His message to the Israelites. We also know that God still speaks through the Bible and the Holy Spirit. Did you know there is one more way God spoke? The book of Hebrews tells us it's through His Son, Jesus!

Jesus told us many things that God wanted us to know, but His message from God was more than the words He shared. God sending Jesus to earth was an important message all by itself. There are seven things in Hebrews 1:2–3 that God tells us to help us understand the message of His wonderful Son, Jesus.

First, God chose Jesus to own all things. That means He is the most honored in all of heaven and earth. Second, God created the world through His Son. Next, Jesus reflects God's glory. We see the light of God the Father through Jesus's life on earth. Fourth, Jesus is the exact copy of God's nature. Jesus shows us exactly who God is. Next, He holds the world and everything together with His word. He keeps everyone and everything in its place. He also forgives our sins and wipes them away. No one else can do this for us except Jesus. Finally, He sat down at the right side of God. That means His work of saving us is finished, and He has been given a special seat of honor next to God the Father.

TALK TO GOD
Thank God for speaking through His Son, Jesus.

So, what is the message God spoke through Jesus by showing us all these things? Jesus shows us God's power. Jesus shows us God's glory. And Jesus shows us God's love.

EXPLORE MORE: What does God the Father say about Jesus in Hebrews 1:10–12? Look it up to find out!

DID YOU KNOW?

No one knows who wrote the book of Hebrews. Hebrews was probably written around AD 67–69. There is no mention of the author in the book, but all the focus is on God. And that's perfect!

Jesus is God's message to us.

A Big Family

So now Jesus and the ones he makes holy have the same Father. That is why Jesus is not ashamed to call them his brothers and sisters. —Hebrews 2:11 NLT

How many siblings do you have? Some people come from families with one or two siblings. Some come from families with eight siblings or even more! And some kids are the only children in their families.

No matter how many siblings are in your family, did you know you have a brother when you join God's family? When you decide to follow Jesus, God becomes your Father in heaven. And since Jesus is God's Son, that makes Him your brother in the family of God!

TALK TO GOD
Thank God for giving you such a big, loving family through Jesus.

Hebrews 2:11 says, "Jesus and the ones he makes holy have the same Father. That is why Jesus is not ashamed to call them his brothers and sisters." If all the people Jesus makes holy are His brothers and sisters, that means you get a big family of siblings when you become a Christian. The great thing about families is that no matter what happens, good or bad, you have a group of people you are connected to who will love you. God created families to support us and help us and be there for us in happy and sad times. Just think how wonderful it is to know that's true for God's huge family of believers too!

How can you be a good sibling in God's family? You can encourage and love your brothers and sisters in the kingdom of God. You can pray for them. You can be sad with them when they are sad. You can be excited when they are excited. You can share what you have with those who don't have as much. And you can keep cheering them on as they follow Jesus.

EXPLORE MORE: What did Jesus say about His family in Mark 3:31–35?

I can be a part of God's big family.

DID YOU KNOW?
One of the largest families in Canada is the Ionce family. The parents were born in Romania and moved to Canada in the 1990s. They have eighteen children.

God's Word Lasts Forever

For you have been born again, but not to a life that will quickly end. Your new life will last forever because it comes from the eternal, living word of God. —1 Peter 1:23 NLT

Do you like getting a new pair of shoes? New shoes look good for a while. But soon they get scuffed and worn out. And as your feet grow, your shoes become too small. New games are fun to get too. But whether it's a board game, or a game for your tablet or computer, games don't last forever either. You might get tired of playing the game, you might lose some of the pieces, or your electronic device might stop working. Can you think of other things that don't last long? What about your birthday cake? That might disappear in a day or two!

When the apostle Peter was teaching Christians about God to help them grow in their faith, he used some verses from the Old Testament book of Isaiah. The prophet Isaiah said that people are like grass in the spring, and their beauty is like a flower. But grass dries up, and flowers fall to the ground. They do not last forever. Then he said, "But the word of God lasts forever."

God's word is the Bible, and the stories, prophecies, and truth in the Bible will last forever. The Word of God is also Jesus. Jesus was with God in the beginning, and He is our Lord and Savior who lives forever.

TALK TO GOD
Thank God that His word lasts forever and that you can live forever with Him by believing in Jesus.

Peter explained that when we believe in Jesus, we are born again, and our spirit will never die. Our earthly bodies will not last forever. If we believe in Jesus, one day we will get a new body, and we will live forever with Him. Things on earth will not last, but things in heaven will last forever.

EXPLORE MORE: Read the words Peter quoted from Isaiah in Isaiah 40:7–8.

DID YOU KNOW?
A perennial is a plant that blooms year after year from a bulb or seed that's planted in the ground. The flowers last for two to three weeks, but they will continue to bloom for a few years.

Jesus's followers will live with Him forever.

The Bright Morning Star

"I, Jesus, have sent my angel to give you this witness for the churches. I am the Root and the Son of David. I am the bright Morning Star." —Revelation 22:16 NIrV

The planet Venus is the brightest light in the nighttime sky after the moon. Astronomers are scientists who study the planets and stars. They tell us that Venus doesn't twinkle like stars do, but it has a steady glow. Venus is called the morning star because it appears just before the sun rises and daylight begins. It's the first light to shine in the darkness, announcing the beginning of a new day.

TALK TO GOD
Praise Jesus for being the bright Morning Star who shines the brightest light.

Don't you love waking up in the morning when it's getting light outside? It's fun to get dressed, eat breakfast, brush your teeth, and start your day. You might be getting ready to go to school. You might be looking forward to playing outside. Maybe you will practice the piano, read a book, or play a game. Mornings are a time of joy and excitement as you look forward to a new day.

In one of the visions John saw while he was on the Island of Patmos, Jesus said He is the bright Morning Star. Like the planet Venus, Jesus is the first light. Jesus created light on the first day of creation, and He is the light that shines in the darkness. Nothing shines brighter than Jesus.

Every morning before you begin your day, ask Jesus to shine His light through you by the way you live. Ask Him to help you do your best in whatever you do. You can also thank Jesus for loving you and being your Savior. Thank Him that He is always with you. Just like the morning light gives us hope for a new day, Jesus gives us hope every day of our lives.

EXPLORE MORE: Read Psalm 148:1–6. Why should everything in the heavens praise God?

Jesus is the bright Morning Star.

DID YOU KNOW?
Venus is the hottest planet in the solar system. It is sometimes called "Earth's sister" since the two planets are similar in mass and size, but there's no way people could ever live there.

The Alpha and the Omega

I am the Alpha and the Omega. I am the First and the Last. I am the Beginning and the End. —Revelation 22:13 NIrV

In Revelation, Jesus calls himself the Alpha and the Omega three times. The New Testament was first written in Greek. Alpha is the first letter of the Greek alphabet, and Omega is the last letter. So when Jesus says He is the Alpha and the Omega, He's saying that He is the beginning and the end—He has always been and will always be!

Jesus has existed from the beginning. Colossian 1:15 NIrV says, "The Son is first, and he is over all creation." As we read stories from Genesis to Revelation, we see how Jesus is everywhere. The story of Abraham and Isaac at the altar is a picture of Jesus becoming our sacrifice. Jesus is like the ladder in Jacob's dream that reaches from heaven to earth. Jesus is like manna in the wilderness because He is the Bread of Life. Jesus is like water from a rock that saves thirsty people.

TALK TO GOD
Thank Jesus that He is coming back someday.

The scarlet cord in Rahab's window represents the blood of Jesus. The story of Boaz caring for Ruth shows us Jesus's love. Many verses tell us Jesus would come from David's family. Psalm 23 describes our Good Shepherd. Isaiah talks about Jesus's birth and life and the meaningful names He would be called.

Jesus fulfills the prophecies of the Old Testament prophets. The Gospels tell about Jesus's miracles, parables, His death, and His resurrection. The rest of the New Testament tells how Christians spread the good news throughout the world. And in Revelation we learn that Jesus is coming back to be our King. He will reign forever as the Lamb who gave His life for the world. Jesus is the Alpha and the Omega—the first, the last, and everything in between.

DID YOU KNOW?

The Greek alphabet has twenty-four letters that are used to create the Greek language. These letters are sometimes used as symbols in science, mathematics, and engineering.

EXPLORE MORE: What does Jesus promise in Revelation 22:20?

Jesus is eternal.

Glossary

The first time the word appears in this book is listed after the definition.

Altar: A holy place where people may give gifts (sacrifices) to God. (Day 5)

Apostle: A follower of Jesus who was sent out to spread the good news about Him. Paul, Peter, and John were some of Jesus's apostles. (Day 63)

Blessing: Kind words or a special gift from an important person. Jacob tricked his father into giving him his brother's blessing. (Day 9)

Christian: A person who believes in Jesus and follows Him. (Day 6)

Crucified: To kill by nailing a body to a cross. Jesus was crucified. (Day 73)

Descendant: The sons and daughters of a person; family members who are born after someone. Abraham lived after Noah and was related to him; Abraham was a descendant of Noah. (Day 4)

Disciple: A person who follows a leader. In the Bible, Jesus called twelve disciples who followed Him, learned from Him, and told others about Him. (Day 14)

Eternal: Lasting forever, or not ending. We have eternal life when we believe in Jesus. (Day 2)

Forgive: Giving up anger toward someone who has hurt you. (Day 2)

Gospel (books): The books of the Bible that tell about Jesus's life—Matthew, Mark, Luke, John. (Day 26)

Gospel (message): The message about Jesus forgiving our sins. The word *gospel* means "good news." (Day 80)

Grace: The help and love God gives even though we don't deserve it. (Day 85)

Holy: Set apart as very special. God is holy, and so is His name. That means God deserves a lot of respect. (Day 8)

Holy Spirit: One of the three "persons"—along with God the Father and Jesus—who are God. There is only one God, but He lives as one "Trinity." The Holy Spirit is the person of God who lives inside us when we believe in Jesus as our Savior. (Day 1)

GLOSSARY

Israel: The name of a person and two nations in the Bible. God changed Jacob's name to Israel after Jacob wrestled with God at the Jabbok River. The great nation that came from Jacob's twelve sons was called Israel. When the nation of Israel split into two kingdoms after Solomon died, the northern kingdom kept the name Israel to show it was different from the southern kingdom, called Judah. (Day 6)

Manna: The thin flakes of bread God sent to feed the Israelites when they escaped from Egypt. The word means "what is it?" The Israelites asked "what is it?" when they saw the flakes on the ground. (Day 10)

Messiah: A word meaning "anointed one," or the one specially chosen by God. Jesus is the Messiah, the one chosen by God to die on the cross to save people from their sins. (Day 7)

Passover: A holiday remembering how God "passed over" and protected the Israelite babies while punishing the Egyptians. (Day 33)

Pharisee: A member of one group of Jews. Jesus often scolded the Pharisees for just following religious rules instead of actually loving God and others. They didn't realize that God is pleased when people believe in Jesus. (Day 42)

Promised land: A place that God promised to Abraham and the family that would come from him—his son, grandsons, great-grandsons, and all of those following. In Abraham's time, the promised land was called Canaan. Later it was called Israel. (Day 37)

Prophet: A person chosen by God to carry His messages to other people. Bible prophets included people like Elijah, Daniel, Isaiah, and Jeremiah. (Day 13)

Resurrection: To rise from the dead. Jesus was resurrected after He was crucified. (Day 61)

Sabbath: A holy day to rest. (Day 40)

Sacrifice: To give up something as a gift, or offering, to God. Abraham was prepared to sacrifice his son, Isaac. He didn't have to because God provided a ram as the offering. (Day 2)

Salvation: The act of being saved, or rescued, from our sins. (Day 5)

Savior: Someone who rescues another person from trouble or danger. Jesus is the Savior of the world because He made a way for everyone who believes in Him to become part of God's family. (Day 2)

GLOSSARY

Sin: The wrong things people do; disobedience to God's laws. The Bible says the payment for sin is death, but God offers eternal life through Jesus. (Day 2)

Species: A group of living things. Scientists use the word *species* to group living things that are alike. (Day 46)

Synagogue: A place where Israelites (also called Jews) worship God. (Day 40)

Tabernacle: In the Old Testament, the tent where the Israelites worshiped God while they traveled through the wilderness. (Day 8)

Temple: In the Bible, the place in Jerusalem where the Jews worshiped God. (Day 13)

Worship: Telling God that He is good, powerful, and worth our love. We can worship God in our prayers, singing, giving, and the way we serve other people. (Day 32)

Scripture Permissions

About the Authors

Crystal Bowman is a bestselling, award-winning author of more than one hundred books for children and families, which have sold more than three million copies internationally and been translated into more than a dozen languages. She is the creator and coauthor of *Our Daily Bread for Kids*, *M Is for Manger*, and *I Love You to the Stars: When Grandma Forgets, Love Remembers*. A conference speaker, freelance editor, and contributor to several blogs, she is also a regular contributor to *Clubhouse Jr. Magazine*, and writes lyrics for children's piano music. She and her husband enjoy spending time with their grown children and huggable grandkids. www.crystalbowman.com.

As a mother of two boys, **Teri McKinley** is passionate about helping kids understand God's love for them. An award-winning, bestselling author of more than a dozen books for children, Teri's books have been published in eight languages and have reached a wide variety of audiences. She is the coauthor and cocreator of *Our Daily Bread for Kids* and Our Daily Bread for Little Hearts series. Some of her most celebrated titles include *Our Daily Bread for Kids*, *M Is for Manger*, and *My Arms Will Hold You Tight*.

Teri's love for writing began in early childhood, as she often wrote short stories for fun. She was exposed to the publishing industry at a young age as the daughter of renowned children's author Crystal Bowman. Her love for writing grew as she attended book signings and writing conferences with her mom. Today Teri also enjoys writing for moms and encouraging them along with their children. Above all, Teri's heart is that her readers would be encouraged and brought closer to Christ through her writing.

Illustrator **Anita Schmidt** lives by the Baltic Sea surrounded by seven seas in northern Germany. Her passion for drawing started from the very beginning when she first held a pencil. Anita went on to study graphic design, but after having two children she rekindled her passion for illustrating and now can't stop drawing!

Jumbo FUN for kids!

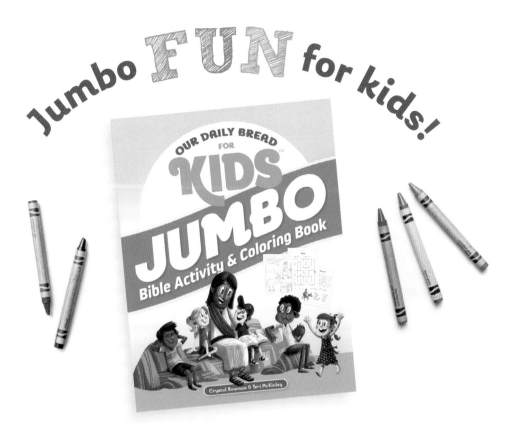

Children ages 6 to 9 will love challenging themselves with activities and coloring pages compiled from the popular Our Daily Bread for Kids series.

Inside they'll find

- ✈ Bible-based word searches, crossword puzzles, quizzes, and other games;
- ✈ 200 pages of interesting and challenging activities;
- ✈ fun ways to remember Bible facts; and
- ✈ hours and hours of entertainment!

Buy it today

DOUBLE YOUR FUN

with both 365-Day
Our Daily Bread for Kids
volumes 1 AND 2!

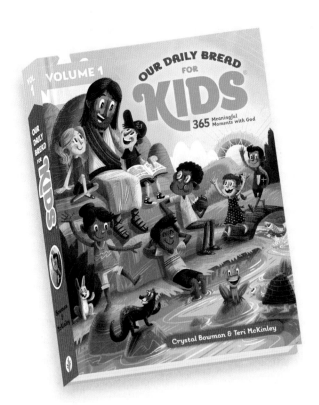

Short and engaging children's devotions, easy-to-remember Bible verses, exciting facts, and fun illustrations make the *Our Daily Bread for Kids* devotional an excellent way to teach your children more about God.

Kids will spot Jesus throughout—from His role at creation, to Old Testament prophecies and pictures of the coming Savior, to the birth of God's Son. With the help of diverse illustrations, kids will see the entire Bible as one big story of God's redemptive plan for the world and learn that God's plan includes them!

Buy them both wherever books are sold.

Spread the Word
by Doing One Thing.

- Give a copy of this book as a gift.
- Share the QR code link via your social media.
- Write a review of this book on your blog, favorite bookseller's website, or at ODB.org/store.
- Recommend this book to your church, small group, or book club.

Connect with us. 🅵 ⓘ

Our Daily Bread Publishing
PO Box 3566, Grand Rapids, MI 49501, USA
Email: books@odb.org

Love God. Love Others.

with  Our Daily Bread.

Your gift changes lives.

Connect with us. [f] [o]

Our Daily Bread Publishing
PO Box 3566, Grand Rapids, MI 49501, USA
Email: books@odb.org